Lecture Notes in Economics and Mathematical Systems

377

Antonio Villar

Operator Theorems with Applications to Distributive Problems and Equilibrium Models

Springer-Verlag

Berlin Heidelberg New York
London Paris Tokyo
Hong Kong Barcelona
Budapest

Author

Prof. Dr. Antonio Villar
Department of Economics
University of Alicante
E-03071 Alicante, Spain

○ 4507769
MATH-STAT.

ISBN 3-540-55087-9 Springer-Verlag Berlin Heidelberg New York
ISBN 0-387-55087-9 Springer-Verlag New York Berlin Heidelberg

Typesetting: Camera ready by author
Printing and binding: Druckhaus Beltz, Hemsbach/Bergstr.
42/3140-543210 - Printed on acid-free paper

"Some of the so-called technical issues are really of the essence of the so-called deep issues and you really can't separate them at all. Each one illuminates the other. In fact they fuse together and in some cases they're identical."

K. J. ARROW

(Social Choice and Welfare, n° 1, 1987)

FOREWORD

Presentation

Many economic problems, as equilibrium models, input-output analysis, rational behaviour, etc., are usually modelled in terms of operators in Euclidean spaces. This monograph deals with the analysis of a number of formal problems involving this kind of operators (with particular reference to complementarity problems and variational inequalities), and their applications to distributive problems and equilibrium models. Thus the purpose of this work is to provide a set of new results on the solvability of those problems, and a number of economic applications that will illustrate the interest of these results in economics.

It is worth stressing from the very begining that our analysis concentrates on the existence (and in some cases optimality) of solutions. That is what is meant here by *solvability* (in particular, nothing will be said with respect to the uniqueness, stability, sensitivity analysis or computation of solutions).

The results on the solvability of operator problems presented here, were actually arrived at as a way of solving specific economic models. Yet we are going to relate this case by somehow reversing the way it happened, that is, starting with the formal results and then presenting a number of economic models which appear as applications of these formal results.

The rationale for this approach is twofold. First, it provides a neat track via which to go through the whole work. Then, because I would like to emphasize the interest of complementarity and variational inequalities problems in economic modelling.

To understand why these formal tools became a central topic in my work, let me say that my first research interest referred to input-output analysis (linear and nonlinear). The existence, uniqueness and comparative statics properties of the solutions to these models were the chief issues. That explains my concern for the solvability of nonlinear equations and related systems under nonnegativity restrictions[1]. When I got involved in new topics (mainly in the fields of welfare economics and equilibrium models), I found that some of them could be analyzed in terms of similar operators. As usually happens, the change of the object required the adjustment of the tools. New formal results were obtained, which in turn suggested new applications. That is the way in which the work has been growing[2].

---

[1] See for instance Fujimoto, Herrero & Villar (1985), Fujimoto & Villar (1987), Peris & Villar (1988), Herrero & Villar (1988 a, b).

[2] This monograph relies heavily on my Doctoral Dissertation (University of Oxford, 1990), under the supervision of Christopher Bliss.

Outline of contents

The work has been divided into two Parts, consisting of two and three Chapters, respectively. The First Part is purely mathematical; it provides the main theorems and analyzes their interconnections. The Second Part contains a number of economic models appearing as applications of the results in the First one.

Chapter I starts by presenting some selected problems involving operators in Euclidean spaces (equation systems, optimization problems, complementarity problems, fixed points, maximization of binary relations, quasi-diagonal images, variational inequalities problems, and nonempty intersection problems), and analyzing their relationships. In that way we try to offer a sort of quick review of alternative ways of dealing with these problems from different perspectives.

Chapter II contains three groups of original results. First we introduce an extension of Z-functions (a standard class in the complementarity problem literature), to vector functions applying $\mathbb{R}^{nk}$ into $\mathbb{R}^n$, and prove the existence of optimal solutions for a generalized complementarity problem. Then, we generalize some of the standard results on the solvability of variational inequalities and complementarity problems for a well defined family of set-valued mappings (either upper-hemicontinuous correspondences with nonempty, compact and convex values, or correspondences which allow for continuous selections); most of the existence results rely on standard fixed point arguments. Finally, the existence of diagonal images in these correspondences is taken up; it is shown that continuity turns out a sufficient restriction for the existence of such points.

Chapter III considers the problem of distributing a bundle of k goods among n agents, according to some pre-established principle, in the presence of consumption externalities. It is shown first that if individual welfare depends on relative consumption (in the standard non-altruistic sense), then any predetermined vector of utility values can be efficiently achieved. Then we prove that any given bundle of goods can be allocated so that the resulting distribution be *egalitarian* (in a sense which depends on the informational framework) and *Pareto efficient*.

Chapter IV considers a market economy allowing for nonconvex technologies. Consumers are modelled in a standard way. It is assumed that the *j*th firm has a closed and comprehensive production set, Y_j. The equilibrium of firms appears associated to the notion of a *pricing rule* (a mapping applying the boundary of a firm's production set on the price space, whose graph describes the pairs prices-production which a firm finds "acceptable"). We show that when firms follow upper hemicontinuous, convex-valued pricing rules with bounded losses, a price vector and an allocation exist, such that: a) Consumers maximize their preferences subject to their budget constraints; b) Every firm is in equilibrium; and c) All markets clear.

Chapter V deals with three different kinds of problems. It analyzes first a generalized version of the distributive problem in Chapter III, allowing for the presence of "goods" and "bads". Then, it takes up the problem of the existence of Lindahl equilibria in economies where agents' utilities may depend on personalized prices. Finally, it presents an application to the solvability of nonlinear input-output models.

Chapters are numbered by roman numerals, and divided into Sections. Each Section is identified by a roman numeral (indicating the Chapter to which it belongs) and an arabic number (indicating the order within the Chapter). Theorems are numbered in accordance with this pattern, in order to facilitate location (e.g., Theorem II,3,1 denotes the first Theorem in Section 3 of Chapter II). Corollaries inherit the number of the Theorem from which they are obtained.

References are given at the end of the whole work, and include only those mentioned within the text. Concerning citation, we follow the convention of giving the author's name followed by the year of publication of the work to which we may be referring.

Acknowledgements

I have to thank first and foremost Carmen Herrero's help and support in writing this monograph; many of the results here are actually a product of our joint work. Luis Corchón, Peter Hammond and James Mirrlees have also carefully read most of the manuscript and made intelligent observations and valuable suggestions.

Some preliminary results were discussed with Parkash Chander, Claude D'Aspremont, Andreu Mas-Colell, Hervé Moulin, Amartya Sen, and William Thomson. All of them made helpful comments.

A careful reading of an anonymous referee from Springer-Verlag has improved the final version. Thanks are also due to Rebecca H. Rippin and Mercedes Mateo, who helped me with the English and the editing, respectively.

Concerning remaining errors and/or misleading arguments, the usual *caveat* applies.

Finally, financial support from the *Dirección General de Investigación Científica y Técnica* (Ministerio de Educación y Ciencia) is gratefully acknowledged.

CONTENTS

0. Foreword

FIRST PART: OPERATOR THEOREMS

I. Operators in Euclidean Spaces: Eight Selected Problems

I.1.- Introduction   p. 5

I.2.- Eight Selected Problems   p. 7

I.3.- Relationships between the Solvability of the

Eight Selected Problems   p. 11

I.4.- Further References to the Literature   p. 28

I.5.- Final Remarks   p. 32

II. The Main Formal Results: Some Theorems

on Operators in Euclidean Spaces

II.1.- Introduction   p. 35

II.2.- Z^k-Functions and k-fold Complementarity Problems   p. 36

II.3.- Two Theorems on Variational Inequalities

for Set-Valued Mappings   p. 46

II.4.- Extensions and Interconnections   p. 54

SECOND PART: APPLICATIONS TO DISTRIBUTIVE PROBLEMS
AND EQUILIBRIUM MODELS

III. Efficient Allocations with Consumption Externalities

III.1.- Introduction   p. 65

III.2.- The Basic Model: Distributing a Bundle of
"Goods"   p. 70

III.3.- Egalitarian Allocations and Informational

Frameworks   p. 75

III.4.- Final Remarks   p. 84

IV. Market Equilibrium with Nonconvex Technologies

VI.1.- Introduction   p. 91

VI.2.- The Model   p. 98

VI.3.- Pricing Rules   p. 107

VI.4.- The Existence of Market Equilibrium   p. 114

V. Further Applications

V.1.- Introduction   p. 123

V.2.- Egalitarian Allocations: The General Case   p. 124

V.3.- The Existence of Lindahl Equilibria in a Model with

Several Public Goods and Price Externalities   p. 130

V.4.- Nonlinear Input-Output Models   p. 135

References   p. 141

First Part:

Operator Theorems

CHAPTER 1:

OPERATORS IN EUCLIDEAN SPACES: EIGHT SELECTED PROBLEMS

I.1.- INTRODUCTION

Generally speaking, an *Operator* is a mapping from a topological vector space into itself. Thus, one of the main features in the theory of operators is the simultaneous availability of topological and vectorial structures. Euclidean spaces provide a prominent class of topological vector spaces, where the theory of operators becomes specially fruitful since in this case we have a vector space with a finite dimension, and a topological structure linked to the notion of inner product.

Operators in Euclidean spaces constitute a standard tool in modelling many economic situations. Equilibrium models, game situations, input-output analysis, rational behavior, etc. are examples of economic problems which are dealt with in terms of such operators. The solvability of those problems usually involves the solvability of some equation system, or some system of inequalities, or a fixed point of an appropriate mapping.

The purpose of this Chapter is to analyze the relationships between the solvability of eight selected formal problems involving operators in Euclidean spaces. These problems illustrate some of the chief applications of operators and have been selected in view of their usefulness in economic modeling.

There is in the literature a multiplicity of solvability results for each of these problems. The analysis of their relationships is aimed at showing how to translate results from one application to another (results which in many cases have been obtained for a particular problem, without linking them with the remaining[1]). In so doing, we try to provide a panoply of tools suitable for the solvability of those economic models which can be formulated in terms of these operators[2].

Throughout the text, vector inequalities will be denoted according to the following sequence: $\geq$, $>$, $\gg$.

---

[1] In particular, "although variational inequalities and complementarity problems have much in common, historically there has been little direct contact between researchers in these two fields" [Cf. Cottle *et al.*, Eds. (1980, p. X)].

[2] This Chapter extends the analysis developed in Villar (1990).

I.2.- EIGHT SELECTED PROBLEMS

Let us take $\mathbb{R}^n$ as the reference space (where $\mathbb{R}^n$ stands for the n-vector space of real numbers), and let $\mathbb{R}^n_+$ denote its nonnegative orthant, that is, $\mathbb{R}^n_+ = \{ x \in \mathbb{R}^n \; / \; x \geq 0 \}$. D denotes a subset in $\mathbb{R}^n$.

$\Gamma:\mathbb{R}^n$ ---> $\mathbb{R}^n$ stands for an <u>operator</u>; we shall also apply this term to the case in which Γ applies $\mathbb{R}^n$ into a subspace of $\mathbb{R}^n$. Γ is taken to be a set-valued mapping (also called *correspondence*), in the understanding that we do not exclude the possibility of Γ being single-valued (in which case we shall usually write F instead of Γ, and refer to F as a *function*). $\Gamma(x) \subset \mathbb{R}^n$ denotes the image of x.

Consider the following problems, which summarize the eight applications of operators we want to deal with:

PROBLEM 1.- (EQUATION SYSTEMS)

Find $x^* \in D$ such that,

$$0 \in \Gamma(x^*) \qquad\qquad \text{[ES]}$$

PROBLEM 2.- (OPTIMIZATION PROBLEMS)

Let $F:\mathbb{R}^n$ --> $\mathbb{R}$, $h:\mathbb{R}^n$ --> $\mathbb{R}^k$, and let D be a subset of $\mathbb{R}^n$ given by: $D \equiv \{ x \in \mathbb{R}^n \; / \; x \geq 0 \; \& \; h(x) \geq 0 \}$. Then, find some $x^* \in D$ such that,

$$F(x^*) = \max_{x \in D} \; F(x) \qquad\qquad \text{[OP]}$$

PROBLEM 3.- (COMPLEMENTARITY PROBLEMS)

Let $D \subset \mathbb{R}^n$ be such that $D \cap \mathbb{R}^n_+ \neq \emptyset$. Then, find $x^* \in D$, $y^* \in \Gamma(x^*)$ such that,

$$y^* \geq 0$$

$$x^* \, y^* = 0 \qquad\qquad [CP]$$

$$x^* \geq 0$$

PROBLEM 4.- (FIXED POINTS)

Find $x^* \in D$ such that,

$$x^* \in \Gamma(x^*) \qquad\qquad [FP]$$

PROBLEMS 5.- (MAXIMIZATION OF BINARY RELATIONS)

Let Γ denote a binary relation on D associating to each $x \in D$ a set $\Gamma(x)$ which may be interpreted as the set of those elements in D which are "better", "larger" or "after" x. Then, find some x^* in D such that,

$$\Gamma(x^*) = \emptyset \qquad\qquad [MBR]$$

PROBLEM 6.- (QUASI-DIAGONAL IMAGES)

Find $x^* \in D$, $y^* \in \Gamma(x^*)$ such that, $\forall \, i, \, k = 1, 2, \ldots, n$,

$$y_i^* > y_k^* \implies x_i^* = 0 \qquad\qquad [QDI]$$

PROBLEM 7.- (VARIATIONAL INEQUALITIES PROBLEMS)

Find $x^* \in D$, $y^* \in \Gamma(x^*)$ such that,

$$(x - x^*) \, y^* \geq 0 \qquad \qquad \text{[VIP]}$$

for all $x \in D$.

PROBLEM 8.- (NONEMPTY INTERSECTION PROBLEMS)

For each x in D, let $\Gamma(x)$ stand for a subset of D. Then, find $x^* \in D$ such that,

$$x^* \in \bigcap_{x \in D} \Gamma(x) \qquad \qquad \text{[NIP]}$$

Problems 1 and 2 are probably the first type of applications of operators an economist meets (macroeconomic models, agents' equilibrium, Leontief economies, etc.).

A specific form of Problem 3 (directly related to Problem 2), is also well known: that in which Γ stands for the n-vector function of partial derivatives in an optimization problem; [CP] corresponds in this case to Kuhn & Tucker necessary conditions for an optimum [see below]. Furthermore, if we think of Γ as an excess supply mapping and of x as a price vector, a solution to [CP] corresponds to a (free-disposal) equilibrium.

Problem 4 is familiar for those who have been trained in general equilibrium or game theory. By letting Γ stand for the Cartesian product of n best reply mappings in a noncooperative n-person game, an equilibrium for such a game is, by definition, a fixed point of Γ.

Problem 5 appears in the context of preference modelling, though it is usually transformed into Problem 2 by means of the representation of binary relations by continuous functions.

Thus, each of the problems, 1 to 5 defines a (relatively) straightforward setting in which some standard economic models can be framed. This is not the case for problems 6, 7 and 8. Yet, they may be regarded as suitable intermediate steps for the solvability of the former problems, as we shall analyze.

From a mathematical viewpoint, each of these problems defines by itself a field of research in which a multiplicity of solvability results exists. Next Section tries to show how one can translate results from one field to another, by examining the relationships between them.

I.3.- RELATIONSHIPS BETWEEN THE SOLVABILITY OF THE EIGHT SELECTED PROBLEMS

For the sake of simplicity in exposition, let us introduce the following definition:

Definition.- We shall say that $\Gamma:D \subset \mathbb{R}^n \dashrightarrow \mathbb{R}^n$ is a **regular mapping** on D, if there exists an upper hemicontinuous correspondence, $\mu:D \dashrightarrow \mathbb{R}^n$ such that, for all $x \in D$,

(a) $\mu(x) \subset \Gamma(x)$

(b) $\mu(x)$ is nonempty, compact and convex.

Remark.- A set-valued mapping is called <u>regular</u> if it contains an upper hemicontinuous subcorrespondence with nonempty, compact and convex values. A particular family of regular mappings is given by those correspondences which allow for continuous selections (this can be ensured if either Γ is nonempty valued, convex valued and $\Gamma^{-1}(y)$ is open for each y in $\Gamma(D)$ [Browder (1968)], or Γ is lower hemicontinuous, with nonempty, closed and convex values [Michael (1956)]). Trivially, a single-valued mapping F is regular if and only if it is continuous on D.

In order to save notation, we shall always refer to Γ although in some cases (which will be apparent) we may be referring to the μ subcorrespondence.

I.3.1.- Equation systems, Complementarity Problems, Fixed Points and Nonempty Intersection Problems

It can immediately be seen that solving Problem 1 is equivalent to finding a fixpoint of a mapping $G:D \dashrightarrow \mathbb{R}^n$, given by,

$$G(x) = x - \alpha \, \Gamma(x)$$

where α is any non-zero scalar, and $\alpha\Gamma(x)$ denotes the set of points $z \in \mathbb{R}^n$ such that, $z = \alpha y$, for $y \in \Gamma(x)$. Thus if D is a compact and convex set and Γ is a regular mapping such that G applies D into itself, Kakutani's Fixed Point Theorem ensures the existence of some x^* in D such that $x^* \in G(x^*)$, and hence $0 \in \Gamma(x^*)$.

Complementarity problems may be thought of as an extension of equation systems under nonnegativity constraints. Notice that in [CP] as $y^* \geq 0$ and $x^* \, y^* = 0$, with $x^* \geq 0$, it follows that $x_i^* = 0$ whenever $y_i^* > 0$. Hence, if either x^* is strictly positive, or $y_i \leq 0$ whenever $x_i = 0$ (a typical boundary condition), a solution to [CP] provides a solution to [ES], with $x^* \geq 0$.

More generally, a solution to [CP] may be seen as a solution to a particular equation system. For that, define a set-valued mapping T from D into $\mathbb{R}^n$ as follows:

$$T(x) := \{ \min_{cw} (x, y) \text{ with } y \in \Gamma(x) \}$$

where the subscript *cw* indicates "component-wise"[3]. Then, x^* is a solution to the equation system $0 \in T(x)$ if and only if it solves [CP].

By linking together the two arguments above, a solution to a complementarity problem may also be regarded as a fixed point of a mapping $H:D \longrightarrow \mathbb{R}^n$ given by:

$$H(x) := \{ \sup_{cw} (0, x - \alpha y), \text{ for } y \in \Gamma(x) \}$$

with $\alpha > 0$. If H has a fixed point,

$$x^* = \sup_{cw} (0, x^* - \alpha y^*), \text{ for } y^* \in \Gamma(x^*)$$

we have $x^* \geq x^* - \alpha y^*$, and hence, $x^* \geq 0$ and $y^* \geq 0$. To see that $x^* y^* = 0$ suppose, by way of contradiction, that $x_i^* > 0$ and $y_i^* > 0$ can simultaneously hold. Then, since

$$x_i^* = \sup. \{ 0, x_i^* - \alpha y_i^* \},$$

it must be the case that $x_i^* - \alpha y_i^* > 0$, and hence

$$x_i^* = x_i^* - \alpha y_i^* ,$$

which is not possible when $y_i^* > 0$.

---

[3] That is, given any two points x, y in $\mathbb{R}^n$, $\min_{cw} (x, y) = z$ means: $z_i \equiv \min.(x_i, y_i)$, $i = 1, 2, ..., n$.

This approach to the solvability of equation systems (resp. complementarity problems) becomes operational when Γ is a regular mapping (in which case both G and H are regular), and there exists a suitable compact and convex subset Q ⊂ D, such that G maps Q into itself (resp. a compact and convex subset Q ⊂ D such that H(Q) ⊂ Q). Then, Kakutani's Fixed Point Theorem can be applied.

This convenient set will exist when mapping G (resp. H) satisfies some contraction property [see for instance Ortega & Rheinboldt (1970, Ch. 5), Fan (1969, Th. 6), Border (1985, Th. 17.6), Fujimoto & Villar (1987)]. It is worth pointing out in this connection that we can let α be an arbitrary continuous function applying D into int.$\mathbb{R}_+$.

Concentrating on complementarity problems, suitable contraction properties on H can be induced when: (i) There exists some $\mathbf{x}' \in D$ such that $\mathbf{y}' \geq 0$, for some $\mathbf{y}' \in \Gamma(\mathbf{x}')$, and (ii) Γ exhibits some monotonic property (notice that both requirements need not be independent). It can be shown that for single-valued mappings point (i) follows in many cases if we assume F to be *order coercive*[4] [see Moré(1974 b)] or *semimonotone*[5] [see Karamardian (1972), Herrero & Silva (1991), and

---

[4] A single-valued mapping F is *order coercive* on D if for each unbounded increasing sequence $\{\mathbf{x}^k\}$ in D, for some index i we have:

$$\lim_{k \to +\infty} F_i(\mathbf{x}^k) = +\infty$$

[5] A single-valued mapping F is called *semimonotone* on D, if for each

Section II,3 below]. The second requirement is fulfilled when F belongs to a well defined class of functions, as it is the case for Z-*functions*[6] [see Moré (1974 a, b)], or asubclass of P-*functions*[7], to name a few [see also Villar & Herrero (1989, Th. 1)]. In more specific cases the same procedure can be applied for non-regular mappings; this happens for a subclass of Z-functions [Villar & Herrero (1989, Th. 2)], and for *isotone*[8] mappings [Fujimoto (1984, Th. 2)]. In both cases no continuity or convex-valuedness is required; the fixed points are obtained from the application of Tarski's Fixed Point Theorem[9].

$x \in D$, $x \neq 0$, there exists some index i such that,

$$x_i \, F_i(x) \geq 0, \quad \text{with } x_i \neq 0$$

(we shall define later on this concept for set-valued mappings).

[6] A single-valued mapping F is called a Z *Function* (also called *off diagonally antitone*) on D, if for all $x, y \in D$ such that $x \geq y$, it follows that:

$$x_i = y_i \quad \text{implies} \quad F_i(x) \leq F_i(y).$$

Observe that if we interpret F as an excess supply mapping, the notion of Z-function conveys the idea of weak gross substitutability.

[7] A single-valued mapping F is called a P *Function* on D, if for all $x, z \in D$, $x \neq z$, there is some i such that,

$$(x_i - z_i) \, [F_i(x) - F_i(z)] > 0$$

The subclass we refer to is that in which this property occurs for that i corresponding to the maximum difference (in absolute values) between x and z.

[8] A single-valued mapping F is *isotone* on D if $x > z$ implies $F(x) > F(z)$.

[9] Tarski's (1955) Fixed Point Theorem can be stated as follows: "Let F be a single-valued mapping applying an order complete vector lattice, X, defined over a ring, into itself. If F is isotone, then F has some fixed point". Fujimoto (1984) provides an extension of this Theorem

Concerning nonempty intersection problems, let us start by the simplest case, and take D to be a unit simplex in $\mathbb{R}^n$, that is,

$$D = co\ \{\ e^1,\ e^2,\ ...,\ e^n\}$$

where co {.} stands for the convex hull, and e^1, e^2,..., e^n, are the unitcoordinate vectors. Now, for each $i = 1,2,...,$ n, let K_i be a given subset of D. Knaster, Kuratowski & Mazurkiewicz (1929) showed that when K_1, K_2, ..., K_n is a family of n closed subsets of D such that, for every subset $\mathcal{A}$ of $\mathcal{N}$ (where $\mathcal{N} = \{\ 1,\ 2,\ ...,\ n\ \}$),

$$co\ \{\ e^i\ /\ i \in \mathcal{A}\ \} \subset \bigcup_{i \in \mathcal{A}} K_i$$

then [NIP] has a solution (that is, $\bigcap_{i \in \mathcal{N}} K_i \neq \varnothing$).

Remark.- Notice that this problem actually corresponds to a particular case of [NIP] presented above. To see this define a mapping $\Gamma : D \longrightarrow D$ as follows: For each e^i, $i = 1, 2, ..., n,$ $\Gamma(e^i) = K_i$. Now, for every $\mathbf{x}$ in D,

$$\Gamma(\mathbf{x}) = \bigcup_{i \in \mathcal{N}(\mathbf{x}^+)} K_i$$

(where $\mathcal{N}(\mathbf{x}^+)$ stands for the set of indices with $x_i > 0$).

_____

for set-valued mappings.

It is also true in this case that if x^* solves [NIP], then it is a fixed point of a continuous mapping [Peleg (1967), Border (1985, 9.2)]. To see this, set

$$g_i(x) = d(x, K_i)$$

where $d(.)$ stands for *distance*. Define now a function, $f:D \longrightarrow \mathbb{R}^n$ as follows: for each $i = 1,2,\ldots, n$,

$$f_i(x) = \frac{x_i + g_i(x)}{1 + \sum_{t=1}^{n} g_t(x)}$$

By construction, f is a continuous function applying D into itself. Hence, Brouwer's Fixed Point Theorem ensures that a fixed point, x^*, exists. Now suppose that the conditions of the Knaster, Kuratowski & Mazurkiewicz's result hold; then, $x^* \in \bigcup_{i=1}^{n} K_i$, so that for some i, $g_i(x^*) = 0$, which in turn implies $g_j(x^*) = 0$ for all j, and the result follows (i.e., x^* solves [NIP]). It can be shown that Brouwer's Theorem is indeed equivalent to Knaster, Kuratowski & Mazurkiewicz's one [see Border (1985, Ths. 9.1 & 9.3)].

Fan (1961) provides an extension of this result for the general case. Let D be a subset of $\mathbb{R}^n$, and for each x in D let $\Gamma(x)$ be a closed subset of D. Assume that there is some $x' \in D$ for which $\Gamma(x')$ is compact, and that for any finite subset $\{ x^1, x^2, \ldots, x^n \}$,

$$co \{ x^1, x^2, \ldots, x^n \} \subset \bigcup_{i=1}^{n} \Gamma(x^i)$$

then, $\bigcap\limits_{x \in D} \Gamma(x) \neq \emptyset$, that is, the set of solutions to [NIP] is nonempty

(and obviously compact).

Finally, let again D be a unit simplex and $F:D \longrightarrow \mathbb{R}^n$ a

continuous function. Define for each $i = 1,2,\ldots, n$,

$$K_i = \{ x \in D \ / \ F_i(x) \geq 0 \}$$

It is immediate to check that when F is *semimonotone* (see footnote 4),

the requirements of Knaster, Kuratowski & Mazurkiewicz's Theorem are

satisfied, and that the solvability of this [NIP] implies the

solvability of the corresponding complementarity problem [for an

application see Bidard (1989); see also Brown's result reported in

Border (1985,9.7)].

I.3.2.- Variational Inequalities, Fixed Points, Complementarity

Problems, Equation Systems and Quasi-Diagonal Images

A solution to a [VIP] may be regarded as equivalent to the

existence of a fixed point of an appropriate mapping. To see this put

$T = \Gamma(D)$, and define a correspondence $\pi: T \dashrightarrow D$ as follows:

$$\pi(y) = \{ \, x \in D \ / \ x \, y \leq z \, y, \text{ for all } z \in D \, \}$$

Define now a new correspondence, $\phi: T \times D \dashrightarrow T \times D$ as follows:

$$\phi(y, \, x) = \Gamma(x) \times \pi(y)$$

Then, if ϕ has a fixed point (y^*, x^*), by construction we have,

$$x^* \, y^* \leq x \, y^* \, , \quad \text{for each } x \text{ in } D$$

$$y^* \in \Gamma(x^*)$$

that is, (x^*, y^*) solves [VIP].

As we shall see in the next Chapter, if D is a compact and convex set and Γ is a regular mapping, by taking T to be the convex hull of $\Gamma(D)$, ϕ is an upper hemicontinuous correspondence with nonempty, compact and convex values, applying a compact and convex set into itself. Then, Kakutani's Theorem ensures that ϕ will have a fixed point [see also Fan (1969, Th. 2) and Border (1985, 9.11)].

In case $D = \mathbb{R}_+^n$, complementarity problems and variational inequalities turn out equivalent. To see this let $x^* \in D$, $y^* \in \Gamma(x^*)$ satisfy [VIP] for $D = \mathbb{R}_+^n$. Then, for $x = 2 \, x^*$ we have $x^* \, y^* \geq 0$, and for $x = 0$, $- \, x^* \, y^* \geq 0$. Hence $x^* \, y^* = 0$. But this implies

$$x \, y^* \geq x^* \, y^* = 0 \quad , \ \forall \, x \in \mathbb{R}_+^n$$

which means $y^* \geq 0$. Thus (x^*, y^*) solves [CP].

On the other hand, if (x^*, y^*) solves [CP] it solves [VIP], since $y^* \geq 0$ and $x^* \, y^* = 0$.

In case $D = \mathbb{R}^n$ [VIP] implies [ES]. To see this notice that if $x \, y^* \geq x^* \, y^*$, $\forall \, x \in \mathbb{R}^n$, then y^* must be zero.

In case $D = \mathbb{R}^n_+$ and $y_i \leq 0$ whenever $x_i = 0$, $y \in \Gamma(x)$, [VIP] implies [ES]. This result is obtained from the equivalence between [VIP] and [CP] and from the equivalence between [CP] and [ES] when that boundary condition holds (see above).

Remark.- The equivalence between [VIP] and [CP] still holds if we take D to be a generic (pointed) convex cone, $\mathcal{K}$, by using the partial ordering induced by the cone (that is, for $x, z \in \mathcal{K}$, $x \geq_{\mathcal{K}} z$ if and only if $x - z \in \mathcal{K}$). See for instance Habetler & Price (1971) and Moré (1974 b).

A solution to [QDI] is a point x^* in D and a point y^* in $\Gamma(x^*)$ such that, for some scalar t, for each $k = 1,2,\ldots,$ n, either $y_k^* = t$, or else $y_i^* > t$ and $x_i^* = 0$. Quasi-Diagonal Images may be thought of as an extension of complementarity problems. To see this notice that a solution to a complementarity problem satisfies $y_i^* > 0 \implies x_i^* = 0$. Thus, a solution to [CP] provides us with a solution to [QDI]. On the other hand, take $D \subset \mathbb{R}^n_+$ and let (x^*, y^*) solve [QDI]; call $t = \max_j y_j^*$, and let e stand for the n-vector all whose coordinates are equal to one. Then, (x^*, y^*) also solves the following (affine) complementarity problem:

$$y - t\,e \geq 0$$

$$y_j - t > 0 \implies x_j = 0 , \; \forall j$$

$$x \geq 0, \quad y \in \Gamma(x)$$

Furthermore, [QDI] can be obtained as variational inequalities in specific domains as can be seen by letting D stand for a unit simplex in $\mathbb{R}^n_+$. Then a solution to [VIP] corresponds to a [QDI], by virtue of the domain structure. To see this, construct the π and ϕ mappings above, and notice that the corresponding fixed point satisfies:

$$x \, y^* \geq x^* \, y^* \quad \forall \, x \in D, \quad \text{with } y^* \in \Gamma(x^*)$$

That means that either $y_i^* = \min_j y_j^*$ or else $x_i^* = 0$, and hence the result follows.

I.3.3.- Optimization Problems, Complementarity Problems and Variational Inequalities

Consider now the optimization problem presented in Section I,2 as Problem 2. The associated Lagrangean function is given by:

$$L(x, \mu) = F(x) + \mu \, h(x)$$

for $\mu \in \mathbb{R}^k$. Assuming differentiability and a sufficient constraint qualification[10], the necessary conditions for an optimum are:

---

[10] There is a number of alternative constraint qualifications allowing us to suitably normalize the Lagrangean multipliers (Slater, Karlin, Kuhn & Tucker, etc.). Should we select one of these conditions, we

$$\partial_x L(x, \mu) \leq 0$$

$$- \partial_\mu L(x, \mu) \leq 0$$

$$x \, \partial_x L(x, \mu) = 0 \qquad\qquad \text{[LC]}$$

$$- \mu \, \partial_\mu L(x, \mu) = 0$$

$$x \geq 0$$

$$\mu \geq 0$$

where [LC] stands for "Lagrangean Conditions", and $\partial_y L(.)$ denotes the vector of partial derivatives of L with respect to the (vector) variable "y", that is,

$$\partial_x L(x, \mu) \equiv \{ \frac{\partial L}{\partial x_i} \} , \qquad i = 1, 2, \ldots, n$$

$$\partial_\mu L(x, \mu) \equiv \{ \frac{\partial L}{\partial \mu_j} \} , \qquad j = 1, 2, \ldots, k$$

Write now $z \equiv (x, \mu)$, and $T(z) \equiv [- \partial_x L(z), \partial_\mu(z)]$. Then, the solvability of [LC] turns out to be equivalent to the solvability of the following complementarity problem:

$$T(z) \geq 0$$

$$z \, T(z) = 0 \qquad\qquad \text{[CP']}$$

$$z \geq 0$$

In the concave case (that is, when F and each h_j are concave

---

take the Slater's one (which essentially requires the feasible set to have a nonempty interior).

functions), x^* solves [OP] if and only if it solves the associated complementarity problem [CP'].

In order to see the relationship between variational inequalities and optimization problems, assume D is convex, closed and bounded from below. Then we may visualize a a solution to [VIP] as defining a point $x^* \in D$ satisfying either of the following alternatives:

a) $y^* = 0$, for some $y^* \in \Gamma(x^*)$

b) x^* is a point on the boundary of D at which we can find a supporting hyperplane with, precisely, normal $y^* \in \Gamma(x^*)$ [since by definition, $x^*\, y^* \le x\, y^*$ for each x in D].

Remark.- As Harker & Pang (1990, p. 165) point out, a solution to the variational inequalities problem may be interpreted as saying that the vector $y^* \in \Gamma(x^*)$ must be at an acute angle with all *feasible* vectors emanating from x^*. Formally, $x^* \in D$ solves [VIP] if and only if y^* is inward normal to D at x^*; i.e., if and only if $-y^*$ belongs to the normal cone $N_D(x^*)$ where:

$$N_D(x^*) \equiv \begin{cases} \{\, z\, /\ (x - x^*)\, z \le 0\, ,\ \forall\, x \in D\, \} & \text{if } x^* \in D \\ \varnothing & \text{otherwise} \end{cases}$$

I.3.4.- Maximization of Binary Relations, Nonempty Intersection Problems and Optimization Problems

Consider now Problem 5, that is, find some maximal element for the binary relation Γ on the set D. For $x \in D$, $\Gamma(x)$ denotes the set of those elements in D which are "better" than x, say. The [MBR] problem consists of finding $x^* \in D$ such that $\Gamma(x^*) = \emptyset$ (that is, there is no element in D "better" than x^*).

Define $\Gamma^{-1}(x) \equiv \{ y \in D \; / \; x \in \Gamma(y) \}$. For each x in D, $\Gamma^{-1}(x)$ is the set of elements for which x is better. Then, by noticing that $G(x) \equiv \{ D \setminus \Gamma^{-1}(x) \}$ is the set of Good Options with respect to x (more precisely, the set of elements in D which are not "worse" than x), the following equivalence holds:

$$\{ x \in D \; / \; \Gamma(x) = \emptyset \} \quad = \quad \bigcap_{x \in D} G(x)$$

Therefore, a solution to [MBR] turns out to be equivalent to a solution to a [NIP], for these $G(x)$ sets. Thus, Fan's (1961) extension of Knaster, Kuratowski & Mazurkiewicz's Theorem, provides sufficient conditions for the solvability of the [MBR] problem [Sonnenschein (1971)].

An alternative approach to the solvability of the [MBR] problem is that of transforming it into some kind of optimization problem. There are two main ways of doing this. The first one starts from the definition of G as a correspondence from D into itself, so that, for each x in D, $x \in G(x)$ and G is closed on $D \times D$. Then, it can be shown [see Shafer (1974, Th. 1)] that there exists a continuous real-valued function, $k : D \times D \longrightarrow \mathbb{R}$, satisfying:

a) $k(y, x) \geq 0$ iff $y \in G(x)$

b) $k(y, x) = -k(x, y)$

Then, the search for a maximal element for Γ on D can be formalized as: Find $x^* \in D$ such that $k(x^*, x) \geq 0$, for all x in D (that is, as a solution to an optimization problem). When D is a compact and convex set, and G is furthermore convex-valued, such a maximum exists, and is obtained as a fixed point of a correspondence analogous to the π-mapping above [see Shafer (1974, Th.2)].

The second approach to the solvability of [MBR] as an optimization problem is the most familiar one among economists. The strategy consists of finding a continuous function $u : D \longrightarrow \mathbb{R}$, such that, for all $x, y \in D$, $u(x) \geq u(y)$ if and only if $x \in G(y)$. In this case, x^* solves [MBR] if and only if x^* is a solution to the optimization problem:

$$\text{Max. } u(x)$$
$$x \in D$$

The chief result in this context can be stated as follows: Let D be a connected subset of $\mathbb{R}^n$, and G a non-trivial binary relation (by non-trivial we mean that int.G(x) ≠ ø, for some x ∈ D). Then, G is representable by a continuous function u:D --> ℝ if and only if G is transitive [that is, ∀ x, y, z ∈ D, x ∈ G(y) & y ∈ G(z) implies that x ∈ G(z)] and continuous [that is, for each x in D, the sets G(x) and $G^{-1}(x)$ are closed in D][11].

Then, if D is nonempty and compact, and G is transitive and continuous, Weierstrass' Theorem ensures that the maximization of binary relations problem will have a solution.

The main difference between these approaches is that the first two ones do not imply the transitivity (or the completeness) of the binary relation Γ, whilst the last one is based upon such a property. Yet, the last approach does not require the convex valuedness of G.

Remark.- There is still another approach to the [MBR] problem (somehow

---

[11] The existence of a continuous real-valued function, u, clearly implies that G will be transitive and continuous. On the other hand, it is well known that if G is a complete and continuous preordering, G is representable by a continuous real-valued function [see for instance Debreu (1959, Ch. 4)]. It can be shown that the transitivity and continuity of G imply that G will also be complete [Schmeidler (1971)] and reflexive. That completes the equivalence.

between the non-transitive but convex case, and the transitive one).
It refers to *acyclic* preference relations. The preference relation Γ,
defined on $D \subset \mathbb{R}^n$, is said acyclic if:

$$x^2 \in \Gamma(x^1), \; x^3 \in \Gamma(x^2), \; ..., \; x^n \in \Gamma(x^{n-1}) \implies x^1 \notin \Gamma(x^n)$$

When D is a finite set, Γ has a maximal element if and only if it
is acyclic [see for instance Sen (1970, Lemma 1*.1)]. When D is a
compact set, it can be shown [Sloss (1971)], that the [MBR] has a
solution when Γ is acyclic and $\Gamma^{-1}(x)$ is open for each x in D.

I.4.- FURTHER REFERENCES TO THE LITERATURE

We devote this Section to provide *some* additional references to the literature. These references do not intend to survey the literature on such a broad area. Rather we shall refer to works that either allow to cover a good deal of the results on the solvability of a given problem (including more detailed references), or to works that illustrate the applicability of these techniques in economic modelling.

The solvability of equation systems (in particular under nonnegativity constraints) and complementarity problems has been ensured in a number of alternative ways, for many classes of vector mappings. Most of them refer to continuous functions arising as extensions of well behaved linear mappings. The literature on the subject is extremely extensive (concerning not only the existence of solutions, but also uniqueness, sensitivity analysis and computational procedures). Here we shall only give a list of references which may be useful as a starting point.

Concerning linear operators, Berman & Plemmons (1979) is a good reference [see also Cottle (1980) for a short survey]. Ortega & Rheinboldt (1970) is a classic book dealing with some of these questions, in terms of iterative procedures (an approach not discussed here). Some selected references on the solvability of nonlinear complementarity problems are: Habetler & Price (1971), Karamardian

(1971), (1972), Moré & Rheinboldt (1973) (which includes an interesting discussion on the relationships between different classes of functions), Moré (1974 a, b), Tamir (1974), Lemke (1980), Ridell (1981), Villar & Herrero (1989) and Herrero & Silva (1991). Some results on set-valued complementarity problems appear in Saigal (1976), McLinden (1980), Rockafellar (1980), Fujimoto (1984), Villar (1988 a), and Gowda & Pang (1990).

Concerning fixed points, there is the excellent monograph by Border (1985), where most of the results with applications to economics and game theory are analyzed. Florenzano (1981) and Ichiishi (1983) are also suitable references. As for optimization problems, Bazaraa & Shetty (1979) is a good reference, among many others.

The maximization of binary relations is a standard way of modelling rational behaviour. Concentrating on deterministic and static environments, Debreu (1959, Ch. 4) or Arrow & Hahn (1971, Ch. 4) are still suitable references for the "transitive" case. Some basic readings on the non-transitive one are Sonnenschein (1971), Mas-Colell (1974), Shafer (1974), Shafer & Sonnenschein (1975), Walker (1977), and the analysis developed in Florenzano (1981) and Border (1985, Ch. 7). Gutierrez & Herrero (1990) provide Lagrangean Conditions in a problem general enough to encompass both the classical quasiconcave optimization problem, and the maximization of (convex) binary relations. Herrero & Subiza (1991) analyze the representation of acyclic binary relations by means of set-valued mappings, and formulate the search of maximal elements as an optimization problem.

A first result on the existence of quasi-diagonal images, concerning continuous functions defined over a simplex, appears in Moré & Rheinboldt (1973, Lemma 4.6). Herrero & Villar (1991) provide an extension of this result to set-valued mappings defined over more general domains, and a number of applications. A different kind of application is developed in Herrero & Villar (1990).

The classical result on the solvability of variational inequalities problems is due to Hartman & Stampachia (1966, Lemma 3.1). They prove that if D is a compact and convex set and F is a continuous function, there exists $x^* \in$ D solving [VIP]. They were also able to generalize this result to unbounded but closed sets by assuming that F is furthermore a monotone mapping with certain coercivity conditions. More general conditions under which [VIP] has a solution when D is a convex cone are provided in Moré (1974 b, Ths. 2.4, 2.5), Chan & Pang (1982), Baiocchi & Capelo (1984), and Villar (1988 a). Notice that one of the reasons why it is important to be able to ensure the solvability of [VIP] on a convex cone derives from the relationships between [VIP], [CP] and [ES] discussed above (see also the next Chapter).

A wide set of applications of [VIP], involving different fields, is provided in the collective work edited by Cottle, Giannessi & Lions (1980). See Dafermos (1980), Dantzig & Jackson (1980), Gabay & Moulin (1980), Harker (1984), (1985, Ed.), Border (1985, Chs. 8 and 9),

Dafermos & Nagurney (1987) for some applications to economic models. Nagurney (1987) contains an interesting survey on the applications of variational inequalities to Regional Economics.

Mathematical Programming devotes two special issues in 1990 to Variational Inequalities an Complementarity Problems. In particular, Harker & Pang (1990) provide an excellent survey on these topics, including theory, computation and applications (and more than 250 references).

Besides the maximization of binary relations, the nonemptiness of the core is probably the best known application of nonempty intersection problems in economics [see Shapley (1973), Ichiishi (1983, Parts 5 and 6), and Border (1985, Chs. 22 and 23)]. Yet [NIP] has also been used in order to prove the existence of competitive equilibria [ranging from the classical work by Gale (1955) till the recent one by Bidard (1989)], and fair allocations [Varian (1974)]. It is worth mentioning at this point the recent contribution by Shapley & Vohra (1991) on the nonemptyness of the core, by using Kakutani's Theorem.

I.5.- FINAL REMARKS

We have analyzed in this Chapter the relationships between the solvability of eight selected problems involving operators in Euclidean spaces. Those problems have been informally grouped into two categories. The first one corresponds to problems which constitute (relatively) straightforward settings for economic modeling (equation systems, optimization problems, complementarity problems, fixed points and maximization of binary relations). The second one refers to some "instrumental" problems, that is, problems which may be regarded as intermediate steps for the solvability of the problems in the first category (quasi-diagonal images, variational inequalities problems and nonempty intersection problems).

The purpose of the analysis of their relationships is twofold. Considered in isolation, the content of this Chapter gives us a number of alternative strategies to prove the existence of solutions to those economic models which can be formulated in terms of these operators. With respect to what follows, this analysis tries to provide a sufficient background for a proper understanding and evaluation of the mathematical results and economic applications in the following Chapters.

Chapter II

The Main Formal Results: Some Theorems on Operators

in Euclidean Spaces

II.1.- INTRODUCTION

This Chapter contains three groups of results on the solvability of formal problems involving operators in Euclidean spaces.

In Section II,2 we introduce an extension of Z-functions to vector mappings applying $\mathbb{R}^{nk}$ into $\mathbb{R}^n$, and prove the existence of optimal solutions for generalized complementarity problems and quasi-diagonal images.

Section II,3 provides a generalization of some of the standard results on the solvability of variational inequalities and complementarity problems for *regular* set-valued mappings. The existence results rely on the fixed point arguments developed in Chapter I.

Finally, Section II,4 presents some immediate extensions, and analyzes some interconnections between the existence of (generalized) quasi-diagonal images, and the solvability of [VIP] established in the previous Section.

II.2.- Z^k-FUNCTIONS AND k-FOLD COMPLEMENTARITY PROBLEMS

We shall consider in this Section vector functions applying $\mathbb{R}^{nk}$ into $\mathbb{R}^n$. First we shall introduce the notion of a *k-fold complementarity problem* for this kind of mappings. Then we shall define a new kind of vector functions which constitute a natural extension of Z-functions to this framework. Finally, we shall also consider the existence of quasi-diagonal images in this setting.

Let $F:\mathbb{R}^{nk} \dashrightarrow \mathbb{R}^n$ be a single-valued mapping. We denote by $\mathbf{x}$ a point in the domain of F. We can write:

$$\mathbf{x} = (\mathbf{x}_1, \mathbf{x}_2, ..., \mathbf{x}_n) ,$$

where $\mathbf{x}_i \in \mathbb{R}^k$, $i = 1,2,..., n$, is given by:

$$\mathbf{x}_i = (x_{i1}, x_{i2}, ..., x_{ik})$$

Then, vector $\mathbf{x}$ can be seen as n ordered points in $\mathbb{R}^k$.

For a given $\mathbf{x} \in \mathbb{R}^{nk}$, vector function F associates a point in $\mathbb{R}^n$ given by:

$$F(\mathbf{x}) = [F_1(\mathbf{x}), F_2(\mathbf{x}), ..., F_n(\mathbf{x})] .$$

In order to facilitate the reading, we shall denote by 0_k, 0_n and 0_{nk} the origins of spaces $\mathbb{R}^k$, $\mathbb{R}^n$, and $\mathbb{R}^{nk}$, respectively.

The solvability of a *k-fold complementarity problem* can be formalized as the search for a solution to the following system:

(i) $F(x) \geq 0_n$

(ii) $F_i(x) > 0$ implies $x_i = 0_k$ [kCP]

(iii) $x \geq 0_{nk}$

Consider now the following definition:

Definition.- A single-valued mapping, $F:\mathbb{R}^{nk} ---> \mathbb{R}^n$, will be called a Z^k-function if, for all x, $y \in \mathbb{R}^{nk}$ such that $x > y$, $x_i = y_i$ implies that $F_i(x) \leq F_i(y)$.

The notion of Z^k-function is a natural generalization of that of Z-functions (see Chapter I, footnote 5), allowing us to work with a domain space that has a dimension equal to k times the image space.

We shall show that Z^k-functions provide enough structure to solve k-fold complementarity problems. For that let us consider the following definition:

Definition.- We shall say that $D \subset \mathbb{R}^{nk}_+$ is a **comprehensive set** if for all x, y in $\mathbb{R}^{nk}$,

$$\{ x \geq y \geq 0_{nk} \quad \& \quad x \in D \} \implies y \in D$$

The next Lemma provides a way of obtaining solutions to [kCP]:

Lemma II,2,1.- Let $D \subset \mathbb{R}_+^{nk}$ be a comprehensive set, and $F:D \longrightarrow \mathbb{R}^n$ a continuous Z^k-Function. Let $x* \in D$ be a solution to the following program:

$$\text{Min.} \sum_{i=1}^{n} \sum_{j=1}^{k} x_{ij}$$

$$\text{s.t.} \hspace{4cm} \text{[P]}$$

$$F(x) \geq 0$$

$$x \in D$$

Then, $x*$ is a solution to [kCP].

<u>Proof.-</u>

First notice that by construction, a solution to [P] satisfies (i) and (iii) in [kCP]. Let it be shown to verify (ii) as well.

Suppose $F_i(x*) > 0$ and $x_i^* > 0_k$ for some i. Define a vector $z \in D$ as follows:

$$z_j = x_j^* \text{ , for all } j \neq i$$

$$z_i < x_i^* \text{ , with } F_i(z) > 0$$

(we can always do this since F_i is continuous and $x_i^* > 0_k$). As a result, we have $z < x*$, with $F_i(z) \geq 0$ (by construction) and, by definition of Z^k-function,

$$F_j(z) \geq F_j(x*) \geq 0 \text{ , for all } j \neq i$$

Therefore, z is in the feasible set and $z < x*$, which is a contradiction, since $x*$ solves program [P]. Hence, whenever $F_i(x*) > 0$, $x_i^* = 0_k$.

Consider now the following definition, that establishes an important qualification of the solutions to [kCP]:

Definition.- We shall say that a solution to [kCP], $x^* \in D$ is **Efficient**, if there is no $x"$ in D such that $F(x") >> F(x^*)$ and

$$\sum_{i=1}^{n} x"_i \leq \sum_{i=1}^{n} x^*_i$$

The following Theorem ensures the existence of efficient solutions for the k-fold complementarity problem.

THEOREM II,2,1.- Let $D \subset \mathbb{R}_+^{nk}$ be a comprehensive set, and $F:D \longrightarrow \mathbb{R}^n$ a continuous Z^k-function. Suppose that there exists $x' \in D$ such that $F(x') \geq 0$. Then, the k-fold complementarity problem [kCP] has an efficient solution, $x^* \in D$.

<u>Proof.-</u>

Denote by $T = \{ x \in D \ / \ F(x) \geq 0_n \}$, and consider the following program:

$$\text{Min.} \sum_{i=1}^{n} \sum_{j=1}^{k} x_{ij} \qquad [P]$$
$$\text{s.t.}$$
$$x \in T$$

Since T is nonempty, closed and bounded from below, and F is a continuous function, Weierstrass' Theorem ensures that program [P] has a solution, $\mathbf{x}^* \in D$. Then, Lemma II,2,1 ensures that $\mathbf{x}^*$ is a solution to [kCP].

Let us show now that this solution is efficient. For that suppose there exists $\mathbf{x}'' \in D$ such that $F(\mathbf{x}'') \gg F(\mathbf{x}^*)$, and

$$\sum_{i=1}^{n} x_i'' \leq \sum_{i=1}^{n} x_i^* .$$

Now observe that since $\mathbf{x}'' \in T$ and $\mathbf{x}^*$ solves [P], we cannot have:

$$\sum_{i=1}^{n} \sum_{j=1}^{k} x_{ij}'' < \sum_{i=1}^{n} \sum_{j=1}^{k} x_{ij}^*$$

Therefore, we shall have $\sum_{i=1}^{n} x_i'' = \sum_{i=1}^{n} x_i^*$.

Notice that $\mathbf{x}^* = 0_{nk}$ is not possible, since in that case we would have $\mathbf{x}'' \geq 0_{nk}$ and $\sum_{i=1}^{n} x_i'' = \sum_{i=1}^{n} x_i^* = 0_k$, which implies $\mathbf{x}'' = 0_{nk}$ [contradicting the assumption $F(\mathbf{x}'') \gg F(\mathbf{x}^*) = F(0_{nk})$].

Therefore $\mathbf{x}^* > 0_{nk}$, and consequently $\mathbf{x}'' > 0_{nk}$. Thus, there must be some i such that $x_i'' > 0_k$. For that i we can construct a vector $\mathbf{z} \in D$ as follows:

$$z_j = x_j'' \quad , \text{ for all } j \neq i$$

$$z_i < x_i'' \quad , \text{ with } F_i(\mathbf{z}) \geq F_i(\mathbf{x}^*) \geq 0$$

By definition of Z^k-function, $F_j(\mathbf{z}) \geq 0$, for all $j \neq i$, and $F_i(\mathbf{z}) \geq 0$ by construction. That is, $\mathbf{z} \in T$. Yet, since $\mathbf{z} < \mathbf{x}''$ we have,

$$\sum_{i=1}^{n} \sum_{j=1}^{k} z_{ij} < \sum_{i=1}^{n} \sum_{j=1}^{k} x_{ij}'' = \sum_{i=1}^{n} \sum_{j=1}^{k} x_{ij}^*$$

But this contradicts the minimality of $\mathbf{x}^*$. Therefore, such an $\mathbf{x}''$ cannot exist.

Theorem II,2,1 says that when we select among the solutions to [kCP] those solving program [P] we are selecting efficient solutions.

The following Corollary turns out immediate:

Corollary II,2,1,1.- Let $D \subset \mathbb{R}_+^{nk}$ be a comprehensive set, and $F:D \longrightarrow \mathbb{R}^n$ a continuous Z^k-function on D. Suppose that there exists $x' \in D$ such that $F(x') \geq 0$, and that $F(0_{nk}) \ll 0$. Then, the k-fold complementarity problem [kCP] has an efficient solution, $x* \in D$, with $F(x*) = 0$.

<u>Proof.-</u>

By Theorem II,2,1, this [kCP] has an efficient solution x^*. Now simply observe that, by Definition of Z^k-function, for every x in D, $x_i = 0_k$ implies $F_i(x) \leq F_i(0_{nk}) < 0$. Hence, we cannot have $x_i^* = 0_k$ and consequently $F(x^*) = 0$. ∎

Consider now the following definitions:

Definition.- Let $F:D \subset \mathbb{R}^{nk} \dashrightarrow \mathbb{R}^n$ be a single-valued mapping. We shall say that F has a **k-fold quasi-diagonal image** (resp. a **k-fold diagonal image**), at $x^* \in D$, if

$$F_i(x^*) > F_j(x^*) \implies x_i^* = 0_k$$

(resp. $F_i(x^*) = F_j(x^*)$, for all $i,j = 1,2,\ldots,n$)

This definition is also a natural extension of that in Section I,2, for F applying $\mathbb{R}^{nk}$ into $\mathbb{R}^n$.

Definition.- Let $F:\mathbb{R}^{nk} \dashrightarrow \mathbb{R}^n$ be a single-valued mapping, and let $D \subset \mathbb{R}^{nk}$. We shall say that a point x^* is **Pareto Optimal** in D, if $x^* \in D$, and there is no $x' \in D$ such that $F(x') \gg F(x^*)$.

The next Corollary provides a connection between k-fold complementarity problems and k-fold quasi-diagonal images, with an interesting qualification:

Corollary II,2,1,2.- Let $D \subset \mathbb{R}^{nk}_+$ be a comprehensive and compact set, and $F:D \dashrightarrow \mathbb{R}^n$ a continuous Z^k-function. Then, F has a k-fold quasi-diagonal image for some $x* \in D$, which is Pareto optimal. If, furthermore, $F(x*) \gg F(0_{nk})$, then F has a Pareto Optimal k-fold diagonal image at $x*$.

Proof.-

Let $g:D \dashrightarrow \mathbb{R}$ be a function defined by:

$$g(x) = \min_{j}\{ F_j(x) \}$$

and let x' be a solution to the following program:

Max. $g(x)$

s.t.

$x \in D$

(which exists, since g is continuous and D is nonempty and compact).

Call $\alpha = g(x')$, and let e be a point in $\mathbb{R}^n$ all whose coordinates are equal to one. Define now $G(x, \alpha) = F(x) - \alpha e$, for each x in D, and consider the following [kCP]:

$$G(x, \alpha) \geq 0$$

$$G_i(x, \alpha) > 0 \implies x_i = 0_k$$

$$x \geq 0_{nk}$$

Observe that G is a continuous Z^k-function and that the set of points in D such that $G(x, \alpha) \geq 0$ is nonempty. Furthermore, D is a comprehensive set. Therefore, we can apply Theorem II,2,1 which ensures that there exists $x^* \in D$ solving [kCP]. By construction this solution corresponds to a k-fold quasi-diagonal image of F.

Suppose now there exists $y \in D$ such that $F(y) \gg F(x*)$. Call $h = \min_j F_j(y)$, define $G(x, h) = F(x) - he$, and solve the following [kCP]:

$$G(x, h) \geq 0$$

$$G_i(x, h) > 0 \implies x_i = 0_k$$

$$x \geq 0_{nk}$$

Again, Theorem II,2,1 ensures that a solution $x'' \in D$ to this problem exists and by construction, this solution turns out a k-fold quasi-diagonal image. But this is a contradiction, since

$$\min_j F_j(x'') \geq h > \alpha = \max_{x \in D} [\min_j \{ F_j(x) \}]$$

Therefore, x^* must be Pareto optimal.

In case $F(x*) \gg F(0_{nk})$, notice that since $F_j(x) \leq F_j(0_{nk})$, for those $\mathbf{x}$ with $x_j = 0_k$ (by the same reasoning as in Corollary II,2,1,1), it follows that

$$F(\mathbf{x}*) = \alpha \ \mathbf{e}$$

and F has a Pareto Optimal k-fold diagonal image at $\mathbf{x}*$.

Remark 1.- Note that we have used the weak notion of Pareto optimality. In order to get strong Pareto optimality, some additional restrictions on the growth of F should be introduced [see Herrero & Villar (1990)].

Remark 2.- Consider the case of a mapping

$$F: \prod_{i=1}^{n} \mathbb{R}^{k(i)} \longrightarrow \mathbb{R}^n$$

that is, F is now a mapping defined from the Cartesian product of n vector spaces $\mathbb{R}^{k(i)}$ ($i = 1, 2, ..., n$), into $\mathbb{R}^n$. Obviously, when $k_1 = k_2 = ...= k_n = k$, we are back into the setting analyzed here. Yet, there is nothing (either in the proofs or in the definitions) preventing us to apply our results to this case. To see this let k denote the maximum of $k(i)$ ($i = 1,2, ..., n$), and define a mapping $\hat{F}:\mathbb{R}^{nk} \longrightarrow \mathbb{R}^n$ as follows: $\forall \ \mathbf{x}$ in $\mathbb{R}^{nk}$,

$$\hat{F}(\mathbf{x}) \equiv F[y(\mathbf{x})]$$

(where $y(\mathbf{x})$ denotes the projection of $\mathbf{x}$ on $\prod_{i=1}^{n} \mathbb{R}^{k(i)}$). Then, all th results can be applied on $\hat{F}$ and then immediately translated to F.

Remark 3.- Let $x^o \in \mathbb{R}^{nk}$ stand for an arbitrary reference point. We shall say that $x^* \in \mathbb{R}^{nk}$ solves a *k fold affine complementarity problem*, if:

    (i) $F(x^*) \geq 0_n$

    (ii) $F_i(x^*) > 0$ implies $x_i^* = x_i^o$ [kaCP]

    (iii) $x^* \geq x^o$

Now, call $D \subset \mathbb{R}^{nk}$ a **comprehensive set** if for all x, y, in $\mathbb{R}^{nk}$,

$$\{ x \geq y \geq x^o \ \& \ x \in D \} \implies y \in D$$

It is immediate to check that all the results in this Section can be readily extended to k-fold affine complementarity problems.

II.3.- TWO THEOREMS ON VARIATIONAL INEQUALITIES FOR SET-VALUED MAPPINGS[1]

This Section contains two theorems that extend some of the standard results on the solvability of variational inequalities problems for regular set-valued mappings[2], with applications to the solvability of complementarity problems.

Let D stand for a subset in $\mathbb{R}^n$, and $\Gamma:D \dashrightarrow \mathbb{R}^n$ for a set-valued mapping. The next Theorem provides an extension of Hartman & Stampachia's (1966) result for regular mappings:

THEOREM II,3,1.- Let D be a compact and convex subset of $\mathbb{R}^n$, and $\Gamma:D \dashrightarrow \mathbb{R}^n$ a regular correspondence. Then there exist points $x* \in D$, $y* \in \Gamma(x*)$ such that,

$$(x - x*) \, y* \geq 0 \quad,$$

for all $x \in D$

Proof.-

Let μ be an upper hemicontinuous subcorrespondence of Γ, with

---

[1] The results in this Section essentially correspond to those in Villar (1988 a).

[2] Those correspondences from $D \subset \mathbb{R}^n$ into $\mathbb{R}^n$ containing an upper hemicontinuous subcorrespondence, with nonempty, compact and convex values.

nonempty, compact and convex values, and let $T = \mu(D)$. Since D is compact, T will be a compact set [see for instance Border (1985, 11.16)]. Let Co(T) denote the convex hull of T. By construction Co(T) is a compact and convex set. Now define a correspondence $\pi:Co(T) \rightarrow D$ as follows:

$$\pi(y) = \{ x \in D \ / \ x \ y \leq z \ y \ , \ \forall \ z \in D \}$$

Clearly π is a nonempty, convex-valued correspondence. Furthermore, π is upper hemicontinuous.

Define now a new correspondence, ϕ from $D \times Co(T)$ into itself as follows:

$$\phi(x, y) = \pi(y) \times \mu(x)$$

By construction, ϕ is an upper-hemicontinuous correspondence with nonempty, compact and convex values, applying a compact and convex set into itself. Thus, Kakutani's Fixed Point Theorem applies, and there exists $(x^*, y^*) \in \phi(x^*, y^*)$, that is,

$$x^* \in \pi(y^*), \qquad y^* \in \mu(x^*) \subset \Gamma(x^*)$$

By definition of π we have:

$$x^* \ y^* = \text{min. } z \ y^* \ , \ z \in D$$

and hence the result follows.

Let now $S(\beta)$, for $\beta > 0$, denote a simplex in $\mathbb{R}^n$, given by

$$S(\beta) = \{ x \in \mathbb{R}_+^n \ / \ \sum_{i=1}^{n} x_i = \beta \}$$

and consider the following definition, that extends the notion of semimonotone functions [see Karamardian (1972), and footnote 5 in Section I.3]:

Definition.- Let $\Gamma:D \longrightarrow \mathbb{R}^n$, for $D \subset \mathbb{R}^n_+$, be a set-valued mapping, and let Gr.Γ stand for the graph of Γ. We shall say that Γ is **Semimonotone** on D, if for each $(x, y) \in$ Gr.Γ, with $x \neq 0$, there exists some index j (depending on x and y) such that,

$$y_j \geq 0 \quad , \quad \text{with } x_j > 0 \ .$$

The following Lemma, which is interesting by itself, will allow to extend Theorem II,3,1 to $\mathbb{R}^n_+$, when Γ is semimonotone over some simplex.

LEMMA II,3,1.- Let $\Gamma:S(\beta) \longrightarrow \mathbb{R}^n$ be a semimonotone correspondence, and suppose $(x*, y*) \in$ Gr.Γ are such that

$$(x - x*)y* \geq 0 \quad ,$$

for all $x \in S(\beta)$. Then, $y* \geq 0$.

Proof.-

Define:

$$\sigma^*_i = \frac{x^*_i}{\beta} \quad , \quad \sigma_i = \frac{x_i}{\beta}$$

Then, by hypothesis we have,

$$x^* \, y^* = \beta \sum_{i=1}^{n} \sigma_i^* \, y_i^* \;\leq\; \beta \sum_{i=1}^{n} \sigma_i \, y_i^*$$

for all $\sigma = (\sigma_1, \sigma_2, \ldots, \sigma_n) \in S(1)$. But this is only possible if

$$x^* \, y^* = \beta \min_j y_j^*$$

that is, either $y_i^* = \min_j y_j^*$, or else, $\sigma_i^* = x_i^* = 0$.

Now, since Γ is semimonotone on $S(\beta)$ we can take a component in x^*, say $x_i^* > 0$ such that $y_i^* \geq 0$. Thus, by construction,

$$y_j^* \geq y_i^* \geq 0 \, , \quad \forall \, j$$

$\blacksquare$

From Theorem II,3,1 and Lemma II,3,1 the following Corollary is obtained:

Corollary II,3,1,1.- Let $\Gamma : S(\beta) \longrightarrow \mathbb{R}^n$ be a **regular and semimonotone correspondence. Then there exists $(x*, y*)$ in Gr.Γ with $y* \geq 0$.**

Remark.- This Corollary may be interpreted as an extension of the so-called Gale-Nikaido's Lemma [see Gale (1955), Nikaido (1956)]. Semimonotonicity is a weaker restriction than assuming that $x \, y \geq 0$, for all x in $S(\beta)$, all y in $\Gamma(x)$.

THEOREM II,3,2.- Let $\Gamma:\mathbb{R}^n_+ \dashrightarrow \mathbb{R}^n$ be a regular correspondence, and suppose Γ is semimonotone on a simplex $S(\beta)$, for some $\beta > 0$. Then, there exist $x* \in \mathbb{R}^n_+$, $y* \in \Gamma(x*)$ such that,

$$(x - x*) \, y* \geq 0$$

for all $x \in \mathbb{R}^n_+$.

Proof.-

Let $D = \{ \, x \in \mathbb{R}^n_+ \, / \, \sum_{i=1}^{n} x_i \leq \beta \}$. By Theorem II,3,1 there exist $x* \in D$, $y* \in \Gamma(x*)$ such that $(x - x*) \, y* \geq 0$, for all x in D. Suppose first that $\sum_{i=1}^{n} x*_i < \beta$. Then, for any $x \in \{ \, \mathbb{R}^n_+ \setminus D \, \}$, choose $\tau \in (0, 1)$ so that

$$z = \tau \, x + (1-\tau) \, x*$$

lies in D. Thus,

$$0 \leq (z - x*) \, y* = \tau(x - x*) \, y*$$

and, consequently, the condition is satisfied.

Let now $\sum_{i=1}^{n} x*_i = \beta$. Then, for any $x \in \{ \, \mathbb{R}^n_+ \setminus D \, \}$ there exists $x' \in D$ such that, $x' = \lambda \, x$, for $0 < \lambda < 1$. Hence, $\lambda \, x \, y* \geq x* \, y*$.

Now, since $(x*, y*) \in Gr.\Gamma$ and satisfy $(x - x*)y* \geq 0$ for all x in $S(\beta)$, Lemma II,3,1 ensures that $y* \geq 0$. Therefore, it follows that

$$x \, y* \geq \lambda \, x \, y* \geq x* \, y*$$

The next Corollary makes explicit the result on the solvability of complementarity problems in Theorem II,3,2, and provides an additional qualification.

Corollary II,3,2,1.- Let $\Gamma:\mathbb{R}_+^n \longrightarrow \mathbb{R}^n$ be a regular correspondence, and

suppose Γ is semimonotone on a simplex $S(\beta)$, for some $\beta > 0$.

Then,

(i) There exist $x* \in \mathbb{R}_+^n$, $y* \in \Gamma(x*)$ such that $y* \geq 0$ with

$x* \, y* = 0$.

(ii) If, furthermore, $x_i = 0$ implies $\Gamma_i(x) \cap \mathbb{R}_+ \subset \{\, 0\,\}$ for

all $i = 1,2,..., n$, then $y* = 0$.

<u>Proof.-</u>

(i) By Theorem II,3,2 there exist $x^* \in \mathbb{R}_+^n$, $y^* \in \Gamma(x^*)$ such that

$(x - x^*)\, y^* \geq 0$ for all x in $\mathbb{R}_+^n$. In particular, for $x = 2\, x^*$ we have

$x^* \, y^* \geq 0$, and for $x = 0$, $- x^* \, y^* \geq 0$; hence, $x^* \, y^* = 0$. But then we

have $x \, y^* \geq 0$ for all $x \in \mathbb{R}_+^n$ which occurs if and only if $y^* \geq 0$.

(ii) Since $y^* \geq 0$, and $x^* \, y^* = 0$, it follows that $x_i^* = 0$ whenever

$y_i^* > 0$. But $x_i^* = 0$ implies $y_i^* \leq 0$, so that $y^* = 0$.

$\blacksquare$

Point (ii) in this Corollary can be interpreted in a number of

ways, and constitutes typically a boundary condition. One way of

looking at it is as showing that semimonotonicity allows us to extend

the so-called Fan-Browder Theorem to convex cones [see Fan (1969, Th.

6), Border (1985, Th. 17.6)]. For this interpret $\Gamma(x) = \upsilon(x) - \eta(x)$,

where υ, η are set-valued mappings applying $\mathbb{R}_+^n$ into $\mathbb{R}^n$. The restriction in (ii) may be seen as a variant of that in Fan-Browder's Theorem; even though they are not directly comparable, our restriction is milder for single-valued mappings[3].

The next Corollary puts the same result in another perspective:

Corollary II,3,2,2.- Let $\Gamma:\mathbb{R}_+^n \dashrightarrow \mathbb{R}^n$ be a regular correspondence, and suppose there exists some $\beta > 0$ such that, for all $x \in S(\beta)$, the following conditions hold:

a) $x_i = 0$ implies $\Gamma_i(x) \subset \mathbb{R}_+$

b) For all $y \in \Gamma(x)$, there exists some index j (depending on x and y) such that, $x_j \geq y_j$, with $x_j > 0$.

Then, Γ has a fixed point.

Proof.-

Let $\Theta(x) = x - \Gamma(x)$. Θ is also a regular correspondence, and, in view of b), semimonotone on $S(\beta)$. Furthermore, $x_i = 0$ implies that

---

[3] The Fan-Browder Theorem for single-valued mappings can be stated as follows:

"Let K be a compact and convex subset of $\mathbb{R}^n$, and let f stand for a continuous and single-valued mapping applying K into $\mathbb{R}^n$. Suppose that for each x in K there exists a scalar $\lambda > 0$ such that,

$$x - \lambda f(x) \in K \qquad [C]$$

Then, there exists $x^* \in K$ such that $f(x^*) = 0$".

Observe that by letting $K = \mathbb{R}_+^n$, condition [C] implies that $f_i(x) \leq 0$ whenever $x_i = 0$ (which corresponds to condition (ii) in the Corollary).

$\Theta_i(\mathbf{x}) \cap \mathbb{R}_+ \subset \{\ 0\ \}$. Then, applying the second part of Corollary II,3,2,1, there exists $\mathbf{x}^* \in S(\beta)$ such that $0 \in \Theta(\mathbf{x}^*)$, that is, $\mathbf{x}^* = \mathbf{y}^* \in \Gamma(\mathbf{x}^*)$.

■

Remark.- Gowda & Pang (1990) analyze the solvability of set-valued complementarity problems and provide results which are closely related to those in this Section.

II.4.- EXTENSIONS AND INTERCONNECTIONS

Let $n(i)$, for $i = 1,2,\ldots,$ k denote k positive integers, and let $n = \sum_{i=1}^{k} n(i)$. Define now for each i a simplex $S(\beta_i) \subset \mathbb{R}^{n(i)}$ (where β_i stands for a given positive scalar), as follows:

$$S(\beta_i) = \{ \; x \in \mathbb{R}_+^{n(i)} \; / \; \sum_{j=1}^{n(i)} x_j = \beta_i \; \}$$

Denote by $\mathscr{S}$ the cartesian product of those simplexes, that is,

$$\mathscr{S} \equiv \prod_{i=1}^{k} S(\beta_i)$$

The next result follows:

THEOREM II,4,1.- [Herrero & Villar (1991)]

Let $\Gamma : \mathscr{S} \longrightarrow \mathbb{R}^n$ be a regular correspondence. Then, there exist points $x* \in \mathscr{S}$, $y* \in \Gamma(x*)$, such that,

$$y*_{it} > \min_{j} \; y*_{ij} \quad ==> \quad x*_{it} = 0$$

for each $i = 1,2,\ldots,$ k.

<u>Proof.-</u>

Since $\mathscr{S}$ is a compact and convex set, and Γ is a regular correspondence, Theorem II,3,1 ensures the existence of points x^* in S and y^* in $\Gamma(x^*)$ such that,

$$x^* \, y^* = \min. \; z \, y^* \quad , \quad z \in \mathscr{S}$$

which in view of the structure of $\mathscr{S}$ implies:

$$\mathbf{x^*}\ \mathbf{y^*} = \sum_{i=1}^{k} \beta_i \min_j y^*_{ij}$$

that is,

$$(x^*_{11} y^*_{11} + \dots + x^*_{1n(1)} y^*_{1n(1)}) + \dots + (x^*_{k1} y^*_{k1} + \dots + x^*_{kn(k)} y^*_{kn(k)})$$

$$= \beta_1 \min.\ \{ y^*_{11}, \dots, y^*_{1n(1)} \} + \dots + \beta_k \min.\ \{ y^*_{k1}, \dots, y^*_{kn(k)} \} =$$

$$= \alpha_1 + \alpha_2 + \dots + \alpha_k \ .$$

Now notice that for all $i = 1, 2, \dots, k$,

$$x^*_{11} y^*_{11} + \dots + x^*_{1n(i)} y^*_{1n(i)} \geq \alpha_i / \beta_i$$

since the first part of the inequality is a convex combination of numbers which are equal or greater than α_i / β_i. Hence the equality is only possible if $y^*_{ij} = \alpha_i / \beta_i$ whenever $x^*_{ij} > 0$, for all $i = 1, 2, \dots,$ k, all $j = 1, 2, \dots, n(i)$.

Remark.- The same proof applies for showing the existence of points $\mathbf{x^*} \in S$, $\mathbf{y^*} \in \Gamma(\mathbf{x^*})$ such that,

$$y^*_{it} < \max_j.\ y^*_{ij} \implies x^*_{it} = 0$$

What this Theorem means is that we can find points $\mathbf{x^*}$ in $\mathscr{S}$, $\mathbf{y^*}$ in $\Gamma(\mathbf{x^*})$ such that, for each $i = 1, 2, \dots,$ k, every y^*_{ij} [$j = 1, 2, \dots,$ n(i)] either takes on a common value (α_i, say), or else x^*_{ij} equals zero. Thus in particular, when $\mathbf{x^*}$ is an interior solution we have:

$$y^*_{11} = y^*_{12} = \ldots = y^*_{1n(1)} = \alpha_1$$

$$\ldots\ldots\ldots\ldots\ldots\ldots\ldots$$
$$\ldots\ldots\ldots\ldots\ldots\ldots\ldots$$

$$y^*_{k1} = y^*_{k2} = \ldots = y^*_{kn(k)} = \alpha_k$$

Thus, $\mathbf{y}^*$ may be thought of as a generalized quasi-diagonal image, since for $k = 1$, this corresponds to a solution to [QDI] in Section I.2.

Remark.- Observe that the first part of Lemma II,3,1 contained an implicit result on the existence of quasi-diagonal images (which did not depend on the semimonotonicity of Γ), on a simplex $S(\beta)$. Thus, this Theorem may be thought of as an extension of such a result for the Cartesian product of k simplexes.

Let $\Gamma : \mathcal{S} \longrightarrow \mathbb{R}^n$ be defined as before, and let $\mathbf{x} \in \mathcal{S}$, $\mathbf{y} \in \Gamma(\mathbf{x})$ be given. We shall denote by $\mathbf{x}(i)$, $\mathbf{y}(i)$ the projections of vectors $\mathbf{x}$ and $\mathbf{y}$ on $S(\beta_i)$, $\mathbb{R}^{n(i)}$ ($i = 1, 2, \ldots, k$), respectively. Consider now the following definition, that extends to this case the notion of semimonotone mappings:

Definition.- Let $\Gamma : \mathcal{S} \longrightarrow \mathbb{R}^n$ be a given mapping, and let $\mathrm{Gr}\Gamma$ stand for the graph of Γ. We shall say that Γ is **Semimonotone on** $S(\beta_i)$, if for each $(\mathbf{x}, \mathbf{y}) \in \mathrm{Gr}\Gamma$, there exists some index j [depending on $\mathbf{x}(i)$ and $\mathbf{y}(i)$] such that,

$$y_j(i) \geq 0 \quad, \quad \text{with } x_j(i) > 0 .$$

Corollary II,4,1,1.- Let $\Gamma:\mathcal{S} \dashrightarrow \mathbb{R}^n$ be a **regular mapping which is semimonotone on** $S(\beta_i)$. **Then** Γ **has a quasi-diagonal image with** $y*(i) \geq 0$.

<u>Proof.-</u>

Since Γ is regular, Theorem II, 4, 1 ensures that it has a quasi-diagonal image at some point $x^* \in \mathcal{S}$. By definition, this implies:

$$x^*(i)\, y^*(i) = \beta_i \min_j \, y_j^*(i) \quad \forall \ i = 1,2,\ldots, k$$

that is, either $y_t^*(i) = \min_j \, y_j^*(i)$, or else, $x_t^*(i) = 0$.

Now, since Γ is semimonotone on $S(\beta_i)$ we can take a component $x_j^*(i) > 0$ such that $y_j^*(i) \geq 0$. Thus, by construction,

$$y_t^*(i) \geq y_j^*(i) \geq 0 \ , \quad \forall \ t = 1,2,\ldots, n(i).$$

■

The next Corollary shows the connection between Theorem II,4,1 and the existence of k-fold quasi-diagonal images, discussed in II,2. For that let S^k stand for the cartesian product of k simplexes in $\mathbb{R}^q_+$ (that is, $n(1) = n(2) = \ldots = n(k) = q$, and $S^k \subset \mathbb{R}^{qk}_+$). Then:

Corollary II,4,1,2.- Let $F:S^k \dashrightarrow \mathbb{R}^q$ be a **continuous and single-valued mapping. Then, there exists** $x* \in S^k$ **such that,**

$$F_i(x*) > F_j(x*) \ \implies \ x*_{i1} = x*_{i2} = \ldots = x*_{ik} = 0$$

Proof.-

Define a mapping $\Psi:S^k \longrightarrow \mathbb{R}^{qk}$ as follows: for each $x \in S^k$

$$\Psi(x) = F(x) \times F(x) \times \ldots \times F(x)$$

that is, $\Psi(x)$ stands for the cartesian product of k identical images, $F(x)$. Clearly Ψ satisfies the hypothesis of Theorem II,4,1, and then there exist points $x^* \in S$, $q^* \in \Psi(x^*)$ such that

$$q^*_{it} > \beta_i \min_j q^*_{ij} \implies x^*_{ij} = 0$$

By construction,

$$q^* = [\ F(x^*),\ F(x^*),\ \ldots,\ F(x^*)\ ]$$

Hence the result follows.

The next result is the counterpart of Theorem II,3,2 for this more general setting. Here again $n = n(1) + n(2) + \ldots + n(k)$.

THEOREM II,4,2.- Let $\Gamma:\mathbb{R}^n_+ \longrightarrow \mathbb{R}^n$ be a regular correspondence, and suppose that for some positive scalars β_1, β_2, ..., β_k, Γ is semimonotone on $S(\beta_i)$, for all i. Then, there exists a pair $(x^*, y^*) \in Gr\Gamma$ such that:

$$y^*(i) \geq 0$$

$$x^*(i)\ y^*(i) = 0.$$

for each $i = 1,2,\ldots,k$.

Proof.-

Let $D(i) = \{ x(i) \in \mathbb{R}_+^{n(i)} / \sum_{j=1}^{n(i)} x_j \leq \beta_i \}$, and $D = \prod_{i=1}^{k} D(i)$.

Since Γ is a regular mapping, Theorem II, 3, 1 shows the existence of points $x^* \in D$, $y^* \in \Gamma(x^*)$ such that $(x - x^*) y^* \geq 0$, for all x in D. Let $K = \{ 1, 2, ..., k \}$ and denote by $I \subset K$ the set of indices for which $\sum_{j=1}^{n(i)} x_j^*(i) < \beta_i$. Then, for each $x \in \{ \mathbb{R}_+^n \setminus D \}$, every $i \in I$, $r \in K \setminus I$, choose τ_i, $0 < \tau_i < 1$, λ_r, $0 < \lambda_r < 1$, so that

$$z(i) = \tau_i\, x(i) + (1-\tau_i)\, x^*(i)$$

lies in $D(i)$, for every $i \in I$, and

$$x'(r) = \lambda_r\, x(r)$$

for some $x'(r) \in D(r)$, every $r \in K \setminus I$.

Thus, $\forall\, i \in I$,

$$0 \leq [z(i) - x^*(i)]\, y^*(i) = \tau_i[x(i) - x^*(i)]\, y^*(i)$$

and, consequently, the condition is satisfied for these subvectors.

Analogously, $\forall\, r \in K \setminus I$, $\lambda_r\, x(r)\, y^*(r) \geq x^*(r)\, y^*(r)$.

Now, since $(x^*, y^*) \in \mathrm{Gr}.\Gamma$ and satisfies $(x - x^*)y^* \geq 0$ for all x in $\mathscr{G}$, Lemma II,3,1 ensures that $y^*(r) \geq 0$. Therefore, it follows that

$$x(r)\, y^*(r) \geq \lambda_r\, x(r)\, y^*(r) \geq x^*(r)\, y^*(r)$$

That is,

$$(x - x^*)\, y^* \geq 0 \qquad ,$$

for all $x \in \mathbb{R}_+^n$, which in view of (i) of Corollary II,3,2,1, implies:

$$y^*(i) \;\geq\; 0$$

$$x^*(i)\, y^*(i) = 0$$

for each i = 1, 2, ..., k.

■

Theorem II,4,2 ensures the enxistence of solutions to a generalized class of complementarity problems in which complementarity restrictions are defined within each relevant subspace.

SECOND PART:

APPLICATIONS TO DISTRIBUTIVE PROBLEMS AND EQUILIBRIUM MODELS

CHAPTER III:

EFFICIENT ALLOCATIONS WITH CONSUMPTION EXTERNALITIES

III.1.- INTRODUCTION

The purpose of this Chapter is to analyze a distributive problem in which a planner has to allocate a bundle of commodities among a group of agents[1]. Commodities may include both "goods" (goods and services, facilities, etc.) and "bads" (efforts, taxes, etc.), although we shall concentrate on the case of goods. Agents may be households, social groups, local Governments, etc. Allocation takes place by means of transfers (or transfers and compulsory contributions), that is, we consider in principle a pure distribution problem. The planner's target consists of obtaining an allocation of commodities that corresponds to some pre-established payoff distribution (that is, the allocation of goods is subsidiary to the allocation of utilities or payoff values).

This is a standard topic in welfare economics, which has been addressed in a number of ways, depending on the equity notions and the class of environments considered. Broadly speaking, we can think of three main approaches to the issue. The first one is that in which the planner's target is formulated as the maximization of a social welfare functional [see Roberts (1980, a, b, c), D'Aspremont (1985), or Sen (1986 a) for a discussion of the possibility results]. Axiomatic

---

[1] This Chapter reformulates the work in Villar (1988 b) and benefits from the analysis in Herrero & Villar (1990) and Nieto (1991).

cooperative game theory, with special reference to bargaining theory, provides an alternative framework for the analysis of pure distribution problems, since it characterizes mechanisms which allocate utility among agents by assuming certain minimal requirements [see Kalai (1985), Moulin (1988, Ch. 3) or Thomson (1989) for some up-to-date surveys, and Hart & Mas-Colell (1989) for a recent contribution]. Finally, one can also face the problem by postulating some *a priori* notion of desirability which captures a well defined intuition of distributive justice [see for instance Thomson & Varian (1985), Baumol (1986), Roemer (1986), Thomson (1987), Moulin & Thomson (1988), Moulin (1989) and the references provided there].

Here we shall follow this last approach. More precisely, two alternative specifications of this type of problem will be considered:

(a) Assume that the planner establishes a vector of target payoff values. The object will be to find the amounts of the k goods and their corresponding distribution, so that the target payoff allocation can be efficiently achieved.

(b) Suppose there is a given bundle of goods to be distributed among the n agents. The planner looks for an allocation that satisfies a well defined equity criterion.

Let us now briefly summarize the chief characteristics of our way of modelling this distributive problem. For the sake of simplicity in exposition, we shall concentrate on the case in which only goods are being distributed.

Concerning the *setup* our model presents two main features:

(i) *The model focuses on economic environments*, rather than on the utility space. In particular, our assumptions will be established on the commodity space and the class of utility functions, and refer to individual behavior. Thus, we depart from axiomatic bargaining theory, where the underlying economic framework plays no role [see Roemer (1988), for some criticisms and an alternative elaboration].

(ii) *Consumption externalities are allowed for*. The very nature of the problem suggests that externalities may play an important role in individuals' welfare, in the sense that individuals may be concerned not only about what they receive, but also about what they receive *relatively*[2]. Thus, throughout the Chapter agents' preferences will be assumed to be defined on the whole allocation space (notice that in general the existence of consumption externalities gives rise to a utility possibility set which may be neither convex nor

---

[2] Interdependent utility functions have been considered in many economic models dealing with distributive problems. Among those closer to our problem are the works of Runciman (1966) and Sen (1976) (analyzing the notion of relative deprivation in the context of poverty modelling), Hochman & Rodgers (1969), Bergstrom (1970), Brennan (1973) and Boskin & Sheshinki (1978) (dealing with optimal redistributions), Schall (1972) and Archibald & Donaldson (1979) (discussing the Two Welfare Theorems in the presence of consumption externalities).

comprehensive[3]).

Concerning the *equity notion* [and with respect to specification (b)], we shall adopt a slight variant of the egalitarian concept (consisting of the equalization of agents' utilities[4]). We shall say that an allocation is *egalitarian* if: a) either all individuals have equal welfare, or else those with higher welfare receive nothing; and b) there is no other feasible allocation with such a property yielding a higher minimum value[5].

---

[3] The convexity of the utility possibility set can be justified "if society were allowed to make randomized choices... and if all individuals have von Neumann-Morgenstern utilities. In absence of randomized choices, ... [convexity] could still be shown to hold in many specific settings, as for example, in a setting where the object is to split a bundle of divisible and freely disposable goods among n individuals having concave utilities" [Yaari (1981, p. 5)].

Randomization in this context makes little sense. Furthermore, neither von Neumann-Morgenstern agents are postulated nor concave utilities assumed.

As for the comprehensiveness of the utility possibility set, it is usually deduced from self-regarding and monotone preferences, and divisible freely disposable commodities. Yet, in general such a deduction is not robust to the existence of consumption externalities.

[4] This notion of equity appears originally in the works of Rawls (1971), Kolm (1972) and Tinbergen (1975), though it seems to have first been proposed by Tinbergen in 1953 [see Kolm (1972, p. 18)]. It is also a standard notion in axiomatic bargaining theory, where it is characterized as the only solution (on the class of bargaining games with convex and comprehensive utility possibility sets) satisfying monotonicity, symmetry and Pareto optimality [see Kalai (1977); see also Roth (1979) for the implications of non-disposable utility].

[5] Notice that what the equality of individual utilities means depends on the postulated informational framework. Hence, by a simple

Besides continuity, we shall introduce the following restriction on utility functions: Suppose an allocation changes so that agents 1,2,..., h receive more commodities, whilst agents h+1, h+2, ..., n receive the same; then, the latter will not be happier. This seems a fairly general way of expressing agents' concern about relative consumption. Notice that this assumption is compatible with individuals who care only about what they receive; what is ruled out is the pure altruistic behaviour (a price which in this context we think worth paying).

Section III.2 contains the basic model and considers the distributive problem under specification (a). Theorem III,2,1 shows that for any given vector of utility values we can find an efficient allocation of commodoties which enable agents to reach these utility values. Section III,3 deals with specification (b). Theorem III,3,1 proves that for any given bundle of goods there exists an egalitarian and Pareto optimal allocation. Section III,3 also discusses the interpretation of these results depending on the informational framework. Finally, Section III,4 considers some immediate extensions and related results.

———————

reinterpretation of utility values on the appropriate informational setting, an egalitarian solution may correspond to an *absolute egalitarian* distribution, or to a *relative egalitarian* one, etc. (we shall elaborate on this point in Section III, 3).

III.2.- THE BASIC MODEL: DISTRIBUTING A BUNDLE OF "GOODS"

We shall concentrate here on the particular case where only goods are being distributed, in order to facilitate the understanding of the model and the discussion of the main results (since it allows to disregard boundary problems which may be present when efforts are involved and consumption sets are bounded from below). A more general model is taken up in Chapter V.

Consider a distributive problem involving n agents and k "goods". $\mathbb{R}_+^k$ stands for the consumption set of the jth consumer, $j = 1,2,...,$ n. Hence, a point $x \in \mathbb{R}_+^{nk}$ denotes an *allocation*, that can be written as:

$$x = (x_1, x_2, ..., x_n)$$

where, for each $j = 1,2,...,$ n, $x_j = (x_{j1}, x_{j2}, ..., x_{jk})$ is a point in $\mathbb{R}_+^k$ denoting the jth agent bundle when allocation x is obtained.

In order to allow for the presence of consumption externalities, agents' preferences are defined over entire allocations. Thus,

$$u_j : \mathbb{R}_+^{nk} \dashrightarrow \mathbb{R}$$

denotes the jth agent's payoff function. Hence,

$$u : \mathbb{R}_+^{nk} \dashrightarrow \mathbb{R}^n$$

is the n-vector function of agents' payoffs, that is,

$$u(x) = [u_1(x), u_2(x), ..., u_n(x)]$$

Remark.- We may think of the *jth* agent payoff function as:

$$u_j(x) = \mu_j(q^o + x) \; ,$$

where $q^o \in \mathbb{R}^{nk}$ represents the *status quo* and μ_j the *jth* agent utility function. Yet, we shall also refer to u_j as the *jth* agent utility function.

Vector inequalities will be denoted by: $\geq$, $>$, $\gg$.

Consider now the following assumptions:

A.1.- $u_j : \mathbb{R}^{nk}_+ \longrightarrow \mathbb{R}$ is a continuous function, for all j.

A.2.- Let $x, y \in \mathbb{R}^{nk}_+$ be such that $x \geq y$. Then, if $x_j = y_j$, we have $u_j(x) \leq u_j(y)$, $j = 1, 2, \ldots, n$.

A.3.- For any $v \in \mathbb{R}^n$ there exists $x' \in \mathbb{R}^{nk}_+$ such that $u(x') \geq v$.

Assumption (A.1) is standard. For non-trivial decision problems the continuity of utility functions is equivalent to assuming transitive and continuous preferences (see I,3,4).

Assumption (A.2) says that when an allocation changes to a situation where some agents get more goods whilst others get the same, the latter will not be happier. This seems a natural way of expressing agents' concern about the amounts and shares altogether.

Assumption (A.2) makes it clear that we allow for externalities, but do not impose them (that is, purely self concerned individuals are permitted). A simple example of this sort of utility functions is the following:

$$u_j(x) = f_j(x_j)\, g_j(x_{-j})$$

where $x_{-j} = (x_1, \ldots, x_{j-1}, x_{j+1}, \ldots, x_n)$, f_j is a nondecreasing function of x_j, and g_j a nonincreasing one (notice that the separability is unimportant).

Finally, assumption (A.3) says that any predetermined vector of utility values can be reached, provided there are enough amounts of goods (this is a non-satiation property implying that negative externalities are bounded). (A.3) is not an essential assumption, but it facilitates the exposition.

Notice that all the assumptions are purely ordinal.

Let $v \in \mathbb{R}^n$ be a given vector of utility values. The problem of finding the amounts of goods and their corresponding distribution so that these utility levels are actually reached, can be formalized as the search for a solution to the following system:

(i) $\quad u(x) \geq v$

(ii) $\quad u_j(x) > v_j$ implies $x_j = 0$ $\qquad$ [1]

(iii) $\quad x \geq 0$

A solution to system [1] gives us a distribution of goods such that all agents achieve their target utility levels, with one proviso:

if some agent ends up with utility greater than her component v_j, then she must receive no goods.

An allocation x^* will be called *Efficient* if there is no $x' \in \mathbb{R}_+^{nk}$ such that $u(x') \gg u(x^*)$ with $\sum_{j=1}^{n} x_j' \leq \sum_{j=1}^{n} x_j^*$.

The next theorem provides a general result on the existence of efficient solutions to the distributive problem [1]:

THEOREM III,2,1.- Under assumptions (A.1), (A.2) and (A.3), system [1] has an efficient solution $x^* \in \mathbb{R}_+^{nk}$ for every $v \in \mathbb{R}^n$.

Proof.-

Assumptions (A.1) and (A.2) imply that u is a continuous Z^k-function. Call $F(x; v) \equiv u(x) - v$. Assumptions (A.3) establishes that for each $v \in \mathbb{R}^n$ there exists x' such that $F(x'; v) \geq 0$. Hence Theorem II,2,1 gives us the desired result.

Remark.- Notice that assumption (A.3) can be dispensed with if we select a parameter vector v, in the image of vector function u.

Corollary II,2,1,1 allows us to get the following qualification of Theorem III,2,1:

Corollary III,2,1,1.- Under assumptions (A.1), (A.2) and (A.3), let $u^{\circ} = u(0)$, and let $v \in \mathbb{R}^n$ be a vector of utility values such that $v \gg u^{\circ}$. Then the equation system

$$u(x) = v$$

has an efficient solution $x* \in \mathbb{R}_{+}^{nk}$.

Theorem III,2,1 ensures the existence of efficient solutions for any predetermined vector of utility values, that is, it tells us the amounts of goods and their corresponding distribution required in order to make people as happy as v. Corollary III,2,1,1 states this result in a simpler way, provided the target utility vector is above $u(0)$.

Observe that this is a rather general result, since:

a) a wide range of consumption externalities is allowed for, and still efficiency obtains;

b) no requirement on the convexity of preferences has been introduced;

c) the result applies for the most demanding informational framework (that is, even if payoff functions do not admit any alternative equivalent representation, the result still holds).

III.3.- EGALITARIAN ALLOCATIONS AND INFORMATIONAL FRAMEWORKS

We shall consider now a more specific (and probably more substantive) distributive problem, where the object is to distribute a given bundle of goods so that the resulting payoff distribution could be deemed "egalitarian".

Let $\omega \in \mathbb{R}^k_+$ denote a given bundle of goods to be distributed among the n agents. The set of *attainable allocations* can be written as,

$$\mathcal{A}(\omega) = \{ \ x \in \mathbb{R}^{nk}_+ \ / \ \sum_{j=1}^{n} x_j \leq \omega \ \}$$

Then, a *Distributive Problem*, $\mathcal{D}$ can be characterized by means of a pair:

$$\mathcal{D} = [\ \mathbf{u}, \ \omega \ ]$$

with implicit parameters n (the number of agents) and k (the number of goods).

Let $\mathcal{D}$ be a given distributive problem. Then define

$$\mathcal{E}(\mathcal{D}) = \{ \ x \in \mathcal{A}(\omega) \ / \ u_j(x) > u_t(x) \implies x_j = 0 \ \}$$

$\mathcal{E}(\mathcal{D})$ consists of feasible points such that all agents have identical welfare values, or else those agents with higher welfare receive nothing. Hence, those allocations in $\mathcal{E}(\mathcal{D})$ where all individuals receive some good satisfy the property of strictly equalizing all welfare values. Conversely, any feasible allocation strictly equalizing all agents welfare levels belongs to $\mathcal{E}(\mathfrak{D})$.

We are ready now to define the concept of egalitarian allocations:

Definition.- Let $\mathfrak{D} = [\ \mathbf{u},\ \omega\ ]$ be given. A point $\mathbf{x*} \in \mathcal{A}(\omega)$ will be called an **egalitarian allocation** if:

(a) $\mathbf{x*} \in \mathcal{E}(\mathfrak{D})$

(b) $\min_{j} u_j(\mathbf{x*}) \geq \min_{j} u_j(\mathbf{x}),\ \forall\ \mathbf{x} \in \mathcal{E}(\mathfrak{D})$

That is, $\mathbf{x*}$ is egalitarian if it is an allocation in $\mathcal{E}(\mathfrak{D})$ for which the lowest welfare value attainable is maximum. In case $\mathbf{x*}$ is egalitarian and $u_j(\mathbf{x*}) = u_t(\mathbf{x*})\ \forall\ j,t$, we shall say that $\mathbf{x*}$ is a **strictly egalitarian** allocation.

Let now Ψ denote the set of all distributive problems $[\mathbf{u},\ \omega]$ involving n agents, k divisible goods, for all possible (and finite) integers n and k, where u_j satisfies (A.1) and (A.2), for all $j = 1, 2, \ldots, n$.

An allocation $\mathbf{x}^*$ in $\mathcal{A}(\omega)$ will be called *Pareto Optimal* if there is no $\mathbf{x}' \in \mathcal{A}(\omega)$ such that $\mathbf{u}(\mathbf{x}') >> \mathbf{u}(\mathbf{x}^*)$.

The next Theorem tells about the existence of egalitarian and Pareto optimal allocations, for any distributive problem in Ψ.

THEOREM III,3,1.- **For any distributive problem, [u, ω] $\in$ Ψ, there exists an egalitarian and Pareto optimal allocation, x* $\in$ $\mathcal{A}(\omega)$.**

<u>Proof.-</u>

Since **u** is a continuous Z^k-function, $\mathcal{A}(\omega)$ is a nonempty compact and comprehensive set, and $0 \in \mathcal{A}(\omega)$, Corollary II,2,1,2 ensures the existence of a Pareto optimal k-fold quasi-diagonal image which by definition corresponds to a Pareto optimal egalitarian allocation.

Thus, Theorem III,3,1 shows that we can always distribute a bundle of k goods among n agents so that: (i) all individuals getting a positive amount of at least one good will have the same welfare values, with no agent having a smaller one; (ii) if there are individuals with higher welfare, then they get no goods; and (iii) the resulting allocation is Pareto Optimal.

This result shows that the existence of egalitarian and Pareto optimal allocations turns out compatible with a wide range of consumption externalities, in a framework where no assumption has been made on on the convexity or insatiability of preferences, and applies for the most demanding informational framework.

*   *   *

Theorem III,3,1 provides a rather general result on the existence and optimality of egalitarian allocations. Yet, unless the informational framework be properly identified, no real meaning can be attached to the equalization o utility values. Let us now take up this interpretation problem.

Specifying an informational framework means to determine the class of utility functions which are informationally equivalent (that is, the class of utility functions corresponding to the same underlying preferences). In order to illustrate how alternative informational frameworks allow for different (and precise) interpretations of the result in Theorem III,2,1, two cases will be considered here: **Co-ordinality** (or ordinality and interpersonal comparability), and **Cardinality and non-comparability** [for a more detailed discussion, see Myerson (1977), Sen (1982, Part III), (1986 b) or D'Aspremont (1985)].

For any positive and finite pair of integers, (n, k), let $\mathbb{U}(n, k)$ stand for the class of n-vector continuous utility functions applying $\mathbb{R}^{nk}_{+}$ into $\mathbb{R}^n$. An *informational framework* can be specified by determining the set of order preserving transformations, $F:\mathbb{R}^n \longrightarrow \mathbb{R}^n$, such that, for each x in X, $u(x)$ and $F[u(x)]$ are equivalent (what can be written as $u(x) \simeq F[u(x)]$, meaning that both functions are alternative representations of the same underlying preferences).

The informational framework known as **Co-ordinality** can be characterized as follows: for any **u**, **u'** in $\mathfrak{U}(n,k)$, **u** $\simeq$ **u'** if and only if,

$$u_j'(\mathbf{x}) = f^{\circ}[u_j(\mathbf{x})]$$

for all $j = 1,2,..., n$, all $\mathbf{x} \in \mathbb{R}_+^{nk}$, where f° is a continuous and strictly increasing function, applying $\mathbb{R}$ into itself.

Therefore, in this case utilities are ordinal but interpersonal comparisons of welfare *levels* are permitted (since the only order preserving transformations allowed in this informational framework are those which are common to all agents).

Whenever we allow for interpersonal welfare comparisons there is always a problem of interpretation. The most widespread view held by economists is Arrow's "extended sympathy approach" [see Arrow (1963, pp. 114-115)]. Arrow introduced interpersonal comparability by extending the set of alternatives between which individuals are (hypothetically) to choose, so that the set of agents be also in the domain of utility functions. Though other interpretations are possible [see for instance Ng (1975)], this is the one which we subscribe[6].

---

[6] There are still several ways of understanding those comparisons [see for instance Sen (1970, Chs. 7, 7*, 9 ,9*), Suzumura (1983, Ch.6)], though Arrow himself made this notion more explicit in a later work [see Arrow (1977)]. The basic idea is to understand each individual utility function as a *conditional function* of a universal one (where the conditional refers to the specific characteristics identifying

Under Co-ordinality, an egalitarian allocation yields a welfare distribution characterized by the equalization of agents' absolute welfare levels.

We may well think of egalitarian and Pareto optimal allocations as the maximizers of a particular social welfare functional: the maximin rule. Indeed, the maximin choice rule seems the most natural social decision procedure in this informational framework [indeed the only one under certain assumptions, as proved for instance in D'Aspremont & Gevers (1977), Roberts (1980 a)]. Then, egalitarian allocations may be regarded either as distributions satisfying a given ethical criterion (welfare egalitarianism and Pareto Optimality), or as the result of maximizing a social welfare functional (the maximin rule).

Let us call Ψ_{co} the set of distribution problems in Ψ satisfying Co-ordinality. Then, the following statements summarize the above considerations:

    * For any distributive problem [u, ω] in Ψ_{co} there exists a

---

different agents). This notion coincides with Kolm's *fundamental utility* [see Kolm (1972, Part III)]. We have discussed this interpretation problem elsewhere [see Villar (1988 c)].

Our model in this sub-section can be interpreted this way. Alternatively we may think of those utility functions as being some *ethical observer*'s evaluation of individuals' welfare, based on agents' preferences plus some objective data about agents characteristics, say.

Pareto Optimal allocation equalizing all individuals absolute welfare levels.

* Let $[u, \omega] \in \Psi_{co}$. If a point $x* \in \mathcal{A}(\omega)$ is an egalitarian and Pareto Optimal allocation, then it maximizes a maximin social welfare functional.

As for **Cardinality and non comparability**, let **u**, **u'** be two n-vector utility functions in $\mathfrak{U}(n, k)$; then, $\mathbf{u} \simeq \mathbf{u'}$ if and only if, for all $j = 1,2,\ldots, n$, and each **x** in $\mathbb{R}_+^{nk}$,

$$u_j'(\mathbf{x}) = \alpha_j + \beta_j \, u_j(\mathbf{x})$$

where $\alpha_j, \beta_j \in \mathbb{R}$, with $\beta_j > 0$.

Here interpersonal comparisons are not permitted. Instead, relative welfare gains can be compared.

To see this, let Ψ_{cn} stand for the set of distributive situations in Ψ satisfying cardinality and non-comparability, and consider a distributive problem, $[\mathbf{u}, \omega]$ in Ψ_{cn}. Define then two reference utility points, m_j, M_j, for each agent $j = 1,2,\ldots, n$, as follows[7]:

$$m_j = \min. \ u_j(\mathbf{x}) \ , \ \text{for } \mathbf{x} \in \mathcal{A}(\omega)$$
$$M_j = \max. \ u_j(\mathbf{x}) \ , \ \text{for } \mathbf{x} \in \mathcal{A}(\omega)$$

---

[7] Certainly other definitions of m_j and M_j are possible, the only relevant restriction being that $M_j > m_j$, for every j.

For every [u, ω] in Ψ_{cn}, and every j, these reference utility points are well defined. We shall assume that $M_j > m_j$ (that is, every agent would find a profitable way of allocating ω if she were allowed to do it at her own wish). Then, for every individual j, and each allocation x in $\mathcal{A}(\omega)$, we can define the jth agent relative welfare gain by:

$$g_j(x) = \frac{u_j(x) - m_j}{M_j - m_j}$$

Thus, $g_j(x)$ is a welfare index which measures the relative change in the jth agent utility when allocation x obtains, with respect to her highest expectations (that is, we measure relative changes in the Kalai & Smorodinsky (1975) sense, when looking at [u, ω] as an n-person bargaining problem).

Notice that for every distributive problem in Ψ_{cn} this ratio is well defined and independent of positive affine transformations. Indeed, g_j itself is an alternative representation of the jth agent preference relation[8]. Therefore, under cardinality and non comparability, Theorem III,2,1 ensures the existence of a Pareto

---

[8] Under cardinality and non comparability $g_j(x) \simeq u_j(x)$, for all j, by taking

$$\alpha_j = \frac{- m_j}{M_j - m_j} \qquad \beta_j = \frac{1}{M_j - m_j}$$

optimal allocation equalizing all agents' relative welfare gains. This allocation corresponds to a Kalai & Smorodinsky solution, when we look at [u, ω] as an n-person bargaining problem.

To summarize:

* For any distributive problem [u, ω] in Ψ_{cn} there exists a Pareto Optimal allocation equalizing all individuals' relative welfare gains.

* Let [u, ω] ∈ Ψ_{cn} . If a point x* ∈ $\mathcal{A}(\omega)$ is an egalitarian and Pareto Optimal allocation, then it is a Kalai-Smorodinsky solution to [u, ω], conceived as a bargaining game.

III.4.- FINAL REMARKS

We have analyzed the existence of efficient solutions to a pure distribution problem (allocating a bundle of k commodities among n agents), in a framework characterized by the presence of consumption externalities. It has been shown that if we assume continuous utilities and agents who care about relative consumption:

(a) For any predetermined vector of utility values we can find the amounts of goods, and their corresponding distribution, so that those target utility values are efficiently achieved (what may be regarded as an outcome providing an answer to the following question: How *expensive* is to achieve a given welfare distribution?).

(b) For any given bundle of goods, there exist egalitarian and Pareto optimal allocations (a result which admits a number of interpretations, depending on the postulated informational framework).

Let us conclude with some final remarks, which provide further qualifications of the material in previous Sections. In order to facilitate the reading we shall number each of the topics we may be referring to.

1.- The presence of public goods can easily be accommodated within this formulation. To see this, suppose we have k private goods and t (pure) public goods. An allocation will now be described as a point in $\mathbb{R}_+^{nk+t}$,

$$y = (x_1, \ldots, x_n, q)$$

where $x_j \in \mathbb{R}_+^k$ for each j, and $q \in \mathbb{R}_+^t$ denotes the amounts of public goods (notice that since public goods are non-rival, all we need is an additional dimension for each public good).

Utility functions will now map $\mathbb{R}_+^{nk+t}$ into $\mathbb{R}$. The next assumptions provide the counterpart of (A.1) to (A.3) into this setting:

<u>A.1'.-</u> $u_j : \mathbb{R}_+^{nk+t} \longrightarrow \mathbb{R}$ is a continuous function, for all j.

<u>A.2'.-</u> Let $y \equiv (x, q)$, $y' \equiv (x', q') \in \mathbb{R}_+^{nk+t}$ be two allocations such that $y > y'$. If $q = q'$ and $x_j = x_j'$, then $u_j(y) \le u_j(y')$.

<u>A.3'.-</u> For any $v \in \mathbb{R}^n$, there exists $y' \in \mathbb{R}_+^{nk+t}$ such that $u(y') \ge v$.

It is easy to verify that under assumptions (A.1') to (A.3') there exists an efficient allocation $y^* = (x^*, q^*) \in \mathbb{R}_+^{nk+t}$ satisfying:

$$u(y^*) \ge v$$

$$u_j(y^*) > v_j \implies y_j^* = (0, q^*)$$

In this context, we can similarly define an egalitarian allocation $y = (x, q)$, as one satisfying the following condition:

$$u_j(y) > u_i(y) \implies y_j = (0, q)$$

Assumptions (A.1') and (A.2') ensure the existence of egalitarian and Pareto optimal allocations of a given bundle of goods (which now may include public goods).

2.- The results in Section III,2 can easily be extended to the case in which ω contains both "goods" and "efforts", for consumption sets affine to $\mathbb{R}^k_+$. That is, for each $j = 1,2, \ldots, n$, let the jth agent consumption set be given by:

$$X_j = \{ x_j \in \mathbb{R}^k \; / \;\; x_j \geq x^o_j \;\;, \text{ for some } x^o_j \in \mathbb{R}^k \}$$

In this case an egalitarian allocation corresponds to a k-fold affine complementarity problem, and Theorem II,2,2 applies again (see the last Remark in Section II,2).

The case of "goods and efforts" becomes more difficult (and more interesting), when consumption sets are taken to be closed convex sets bounded from below, and we allow for the existence of balance restrictions (that is, the goods have to be fully distributed and there cannot be extra efforts). This more general case was originally taken up in Herrero & Villar (1990), and is reported in Chapter V.

3.- Let us conclude this Chapter by briefly considering the case $k = 1$ (the problem of distributing a cake in the presence of externalities). This case has largely been discussed in relation to the welfare economics of income distribution (let us mention the works of Atkinson (1970), Sen (1974), Varian (1974), Hammond (1977), Crawford (1977), Deschamps & Gevers (1978) as short sample including different perspectives),

When there is a single good, assumptions (A.1) and (A.2) imply that function $u:\mathbb{R}^n \longrightarrow \mathbb{R}^n$ is a continuous Z-function. In this case Theorem III,2,1 can be strengthened in the sense of ensuring the *uniqueness* of Pareto optimal allocations. Other results, concerning comparative statics properties and computational procedures, are also available in this case [see for instance the sensitivity analysis developed for these mappings in Villar & Herrero (1985)].

CHAPTER IV:

MARKET EQUILIBRIUM WITH NONCONVEX TECHNOLOGIES

IV.1.- INTRODUCTION

The standard Arrow-Debreu-MacKenzie general equilibrium model provides a basic tool for the understanding of the functioning of *competitive markets*. It allows us to give a positive answer to the old question concerning the capability of prices and markets to coordinate the economic activity in a decentralized framework. This model shows that, under a set of well specified assumptions, markets are in themselves sufficient institutions for the efficient allocation of resources. This may be called the *Invisible Hand Theorem*, and summarizes the most relevant features of competitive markets: the equilibria constitute a nonempty subset of the set of efficient allocations.

The existence of a competitive equilibrium is obtained by applying a fixpoint argument. The typical strategy of the proof consists of identifying the set of competitive equilibria with the set of fixpoints of a suitable mapping, and making use of Kakutani's Fixpoint Theorem. For this approach to work, one has to be able to ensure that the set of attainable allocations of the economy is *nonempty* and *bounded*, and that the excess demand mapping is an *upper hemicontinuous correspondence with nonempty closed and convex values*. An equilibrium appears then as a fixpoint of the excess demand mapping, on a nonempty, compact and convex superset of the set of attainable allocations [see for instance Debreu (1959)].

On the other hand, the efficiency of competitive equilibria is derived from two basic features. The first one refers to the fact that agents behave as *payoff maximizers at given prices*. This implies that each agent equates her marginal rates of transformation to the relative prices (and hence they become equal for *all agents* and *all commodities*). The second one is that *all non-price variables affecting the payoff function of an individual belong to her choice set* (so that prices turn out to be sufficient information, allowing the exploitation of all benefits derived from production and exchange).

There are many relevant instances in which the Invisible-Hand Theorem does not work, either because competitive equilibria do not belong to the set of efficient allocations, or because they simply do not exist (externalities, asymmetric information, oligopolistic competition, etc.). The presence of increasing returns to scale (or more general forms of non-convex technologies) is a case in point. Indeed, general equilibrium models face serious difficulties in the presence of non-convex technologies, when there are finitely many firms. Such difficulties are both analytical and theoretical and have mainly to do with the fact that the supply correspondence may not be convex-valued or even defined, so that (non-cooperative Nash) equilibrium typically fails to exist. Hence, alternative techniques of analysis and different equilibrium concepts must be applied[1].

_____

[1] See Mas-Colell (1987), Cornet (1988) and Dehez (1988), for a review

In particular, profit maximizing behaviour at given prices and increasing returns turn out to be incompatible with the presence of active firms (since, in this case, the supply mapping will not be defined for non-zero outputs). This implies, that if we want to analyze a general equilibrium model allowing for non-convex technologies, we must permit the firms to follow more general rules of behaviour, and suitably re-define the equilibrium notion. This will, however, imply that the identification between equilibrium and optimum will no longer hold.

The modern approach to this problem consists of building a general equilibrium model which constitutes a genuine extension of the standard competitive one. This generalization of the Walrasian model relies on two major ideas:

(i) An equilibrium for the economy is understood as a price vector, a list of consumption allocations and a list of production plans such that: (a) all agents face the same prices; (b) the consumers maximize their preferences subject to their budget constraints; (c) each individual firm is in "equilibrium" at those prices and production plans; and (d) the markets for all goods clear. It is mostly the nature of the equilibrium condition (c) which establishes the differences between these models (both with respect to each other and with respect to the Walrasian one).

---

of the different lines of research to which these problems give rise.

(ii) The equilibrium of firms appears associated to the notion of a *pricing rule*, rather than to that of a supply correspondence. A *pricing rule* is a mapping applying the boundary of a firm's production set on the price space. The graph of such a mapping describes the pairs prices-production which a firm finds "acceptable" (a pricing rule may be thought of as the inverse mapping of a generalized "supply correspondence"). These mappings may be continuous and convex-valued, even when the supply correspondence is not so, making it possible to use a fixpoint argument (on the "inverse supply" mapping), in order to get the existence of an equilibrium.

This approach has to cope with a number of problems when we come to prove the existence of an equilibrium. These problems, which are ones of technique and of substance, do not exist in the standard competitive world, and turn out to be interdependent and to appear simultaneously. Let us briefly comment on them, in order to clarify the nature of the assumptions we shall meet later on:

a) In the absence of convexity, *the set of attainable allocations* may not be bounded. This implies that some hypotheses on the compactness of this set must be introduced, if we want to be able to apply a fixpoint argument.

b) When firms do not behave as profit maximizers at given prices, firms may suffer losses in equilibrium. This implies that some restriction on *the distribution of wealth* must be imposed in order to avoid difficulties for the survival of consumers (and the *upper hemicontinuity of the demand mapping*). Furthermore, equilibrium allocations will not be efficient in general (that means that the Invisible-Hand Theorem now becomes split into two different halves).

c) Each firm's pricing rule must exhibit some *sensitivity* with respect to changes in production, since an equilibrium price vector must belong to the intersection of all firms' pricing rules (think of the case of two firms, each of which only accepts a single price vector for any possible production plan, and in which both price vectors differ).

d) Finally, there must be *some relevant world different from perfect competition*, but compatible with all these restrictions, to which this approach applies.

*   *   *

The problems for the functioning of markets derived from the presence of increasing returns, were first dealt with from the efficiency viewpoint. The marginal cost pricing appeared during the thirties and forties as a normative solution in a partial equilibrium context. It was Guesnerie (1975) who first showed that marginal cost pricing allows us to decentralize efficient allocations in the presence of nonconvexities (that is, he provided a general version of this extension of the Second Welfare Theorem).

The main contributions to the analysis of the existence of general equilibrium in the presence of increasing returns (or more general non-convex technologies), are relatively new (with the exception of the paper by Scarf (1986), written in 1963). Among them, noteworthy of mention are the works of Beato & Mas-Colell (1985), Dierker, Guesnerie & Neuefeind (1985), Böhm (1986), Brown, Heal, Khan & Vohra (1986), those collected in the special issue of the **Journal of Mathematical Economics** devoted to this topic (vol. 17, 1988) [in particular the paper by Bonnisseau & Cornet (1988 a)], Corchón (1988), Herrero & Villar (1988), Bonnisseau & Cornet (1990 a, b), and Villar (1991).

Following along these lines, we shall present here a model of a market economy allowing for nonconvex technologies. Consumers will be modelled in a standard way (although allowing for a revenue structure more general than that one corresponding to a private ownership market economy). Concerning the production side, it will be assumed that the *jth* firm has a closed and comprehensive production set, $Y_j \subset \mathbb{R}^\ell$, and an upper hemicontinuous, and convex valued pricing rule, Φ_j. A firm is said to be in equilibrium when (y_j, p) belongs to the graph of Φ_j. An equilibrium for the economy consists of a price vector and a feasible allocation where all individual agents are in equilibrium.

This model is a variant of those by Kamiya (1988) and Vohra (1988), and turns out to be slightly less general than that one by Bonnisseau & Cornet (1988 a) [see Bonnisseau (1988) and Bonnisseau & Cornet (1988 a) for a detailed analysis of the relationships between these models]. The main difference, with respect to these contributions, is one of <u>focus</u>: The model has been constructed seeking simplicity and understandability rather than generality. In particular, we present a model which is relatively easier to handle, and provide a more intuitive existence theorem.

The main result of the Chapter consist of an equilibrium existence theorem showing that when firms follow upper hemicontinuous, convex-valued pricing rules with bounded losses, an equilibrium exists, provided a condition on the distribution of wealth is satisfied.

The rest of the Chapter is organized as follows. The model is introduced in Section IV.2, whilst Section IV.3 contains a brief exposition of the family of pricing rules compatible with it. Finally, the proof of the existence theorem is presented in Section IV.4.

IV.2.- THE MODEL

Consider a market economy with ℓ perfectly divisible commodities and a given number of economic agents which can be either consumers (with cardinal m) or firms (with cardinal n). A point $\omega \in \mathbb{R}^\ell$ denotes the vector of initial endowments.

Following the standard convention, the technological possibilities of the jth firm ($j = 1, 2, ..., n$) are represented by a subset Y_j of $\mathbb{R}^\ell$ (the jth firm's production set). We shall denote by $\mathfrak{J}_j$ the jth firm's set of (weakly) efficient production plans, that is,

$$\mathfrak{J}_j \equiv \{ \, y_j \in Y_j \ / \ y'_j \gg y_j \ \Longrightarrow \ y'_j \notin Y_j \, \}$$

$\mathfrak{J}$ will stand for the cartesian product of the n sets of (weakly) efficient production plans, that is,

$$\mathfrak{J} \equiv \prod_{j=1}^{n} \mathfrak{J}_j$$

We shall denote by $\mathbb{P} \subset \mathbb{R}^\ell_+$ the standard price simplex, that is,

$$\mathbb{P} = \{ \, p \in \mathbb{R}^\ell_+ \ / \ \sum_{t=1}^{\ell} p_t = 1 \, \}$$

For a point $y_j \in \mathfrak{J}_j$ and a price vector $p \in \mathbb{P}$, py_j gives us the associated profits.

Each firms' behaviour is defined in terms of a *Pricing Rule*. A Pricing Rule for the jth firm may be defined as a mapping Φ_j applying the set of efficient production plans, $\mathfrak{F}_j$ into $\mathbb{R}^{\ell}_+$. For a point $y_j \in \mathfrak{F}_j$, $\Phi_j(y_j)$ has to be interpreted as the set of price vectors found "acceptable" by the *jth* firm when producing y_j. In other words, the *jth* firm is in equilibrium at the pair (y_j, p), if $p \in \Phi_j(y_j)$.

We shall adopt the more general notion of firms' behaviour, by allowing for each firm's Pricing Rule to depend on other firms actions and "market prices". To do this, let

$$\bar{y} = (y_1, \ y_2, \ \dots, \ y_n)$$

denote a point in $\mathfrak{F}$. Then,

Definition.- A **Pricing Rule for the jth firm** is a correspondence,

$$\phi_j : \mathbb{P} \times \mathfrak{F} \ \text{--->} \ \mathbb{P}$$

which establishes the *jth* firm set of admissible prices, as a function of "market conditions".

That is, y_j is an equilibrium production plan for the *jth* firm at prices p, if and only if, $p \in \phi_j(p, \bar{y})$ (where y_j is precisely the *jth* firm's production plan in $\bar{y}$).

As for interpretative purposes, we may think of a market mechanism in which there is an auctioneer who calls out both a price vector (to be seen as proposed market prices), and a vector of efficient production plans. Then, the *jth* firm checks out whether the pair (p, y_j) agrees with her objectives (formally, $[(p, \bar{y}), p]$ belongs to the graph of ϕ_j). A situation in which all firms find acceptable the proposed combination between market prices and production plans is called a *production equilibrium*. Formally:

Definition.- We shall say that a pair $(p, \bar{y}) \in \mathbb{P} \times \mathfrak{F}$ is a **Production Equilibrium** if $p \in \bigcap_{j=1}^{n} \phi_j(p, \bar{y})$.

Observe that different firms may follow different pricing rules. Furthermore, the pricing rule "may be either endogenous or exogenous to the model, and that it allows both price-taking and price-setting behaviors" [Cf. Cornet (1988, p. 106)].

There are m consumers. Each consumer $i = 1, 2, \ldots, m$, is characterized by a tuple,

$$[C_i, u_i, r_i]$$

where C_i, u_i stand for the *ith* consumer consumption set and utility function, respectively, and r_i denotes the *ith* consumer's wealth. To be precise, r_i is a mapping applying $\mathbb{P} \times \mathbb{R}^{\ell n}$ into $\mathbb{R}$ so that, for each pair $(p, \bar{y})$, $r_i(p, \bar{y})$ gives us the *ith* consumers' wealth.

Notice that in the case of a private ownership market economy we have: $r_i(p, \bar{y}) = p \, \omega_i + \sum_{i=1}^{n} \theta_{ij} \, p \, y_j$ (where ω_i stands for the *ith* consumer's initial endowments, and θ_{ij} for the *ith* consumer's participation in the *jth* firms' profits). Therefore, this way of defining consumers' wealth allows for more general income structures.

We shall follow the convention of denoting with negative numbers those commodities which a consumer may supply.

Given a price vector $\mathbf{p}$, and a vector of production plans $\bar{\mathbf{y}} \in \mathfrak{J}$ [with $\bar{\mathbf{y}} = (\mathbf{y}_1, \mathbf{y}_2, \ldots, \mathbf{y}_n)$], the ith consumer's behaviour is obtained by solving the following program:

$$\text{Max.} \quad u_i$$
$$\text{s.t.:}$$
$$c_i \in C_i$$
$$\mathbf{p}\, c_i \leq r_i(\mathbf{p}, \bar{\mathbf{y}})$$

Let $(\mathbf{p}, \bar{\mathbf{y}}) \in \mathbb{P} \times \mathfrak{J}$ be given. Then, consumers' behaviour can be summarized by an aggregate net demand correspondence, that can be written as follows:

$$\xi(\mathbf{p}, \bar{\mathbf{y}}) = d(\mathbf{p}, \bar{\mathbf{y}}) - \{\,\omega\,\}$$

where $d(\mathbf{p}, \bar{\mathbf{y}}) \equiv \sum_{i=1}^{m} d_i(\mathbf{p}, \bar{\mathbf{y}})$, and $d_i(\mathbf{p}, \bar{\mathbf{y}})$ stands for the set of solutions to the program above for $(\mathbf{p}, \bar{\mathbf{y}})$.

Observe that since consumers' choices depend on market prices and firms' production, we may think of each ϕ_j as also being dependent on consumers' decisions, that is,

$$\phi_j(\mathbf{p}, \bar{\mathbf{y}}) = \Theta_j[\mathbf{p}, \bar{\mathbf{y}}, \xi(\mathbf{p}, \bar{\mathbf{y}})].$$

This provides enough flexibility to deal with market situations in which firms' target payoffs may depend on demand conditions.

Consider now the following assumptions:

A.1.- For each firm $j = 1, 2, \ldots, n$,

(i) Y_j is a closed subset of $\mathbb{R}^\ell$.

(ii) $Y_j - \mathbb{R}^\ell_+ \subset Y_j$.

(iii) For each given vector of initial endowments, $\omega \in \mathbb{R}^\ell$, the set

$$\mathscr{A}(\omega) \equiv \left\{ [(c_i), \bar{y}] \in \prod_{i=1}^{m} C_i \times \prod_{j=1}^{n} Y_j \;/\; \sum_{i=1}^{m} c_i - \omega \leq \sum_{j=1}^{n} y_j \right\}$$

is bounded.

This assumption provides us with a suitable generalization of the standard way of modelling production sets. Besides the technical point (i), point (ii) corresponds to the free-disposal assumption. Finally, point (iii) says that the set of attainable allocations is bounded, so that it is not possible for the *jth* firm to obtain an unlimited amount of production out of a given vector of initial endowments. Observe that *under (A.1) the set of weakly efficient production plans, $\mathfrak{F}_j$, consists exactly of those points in the boundary of Y_j.*

A.2.- For each $i = 1, 2, \ldots, m$,

(i) C_i is a closed and convex subset of $\mathbb{R}^\ell$, bounded from below.

(ii) $u_i : C_i \longrightarrow \mathbb{R}$ is a continuous and quasi-concave function.

(iii) (Local non-satiation) For each $c_i \in C_i$, every $\varepsilon > 0$ there exists some $c_i' \in B(c_i, \varepsilon) \cap C_i$ such that $u_i(c_i') > u_i(c_i)$ (where

$B(c_i, \varepsilon)$ stands for a closed ball with centre c_i and radius ε).

(iv) $r_i: \mathbb{P} \times \mathbb{R}^{\ell n} \rightarrow \mathbb{R}$ is a continuous function such that, for every $(\mathbf{p}, \bar{\mathbf{y}}) \in \mathbb{P} \times \mathbb{R}^{\ell n}$, we have:

$$\sum_{i=1}^{m} r_i(\mathbf{p}, \bar{\mathbf{y}}) = p(\omega + \sum_{j=1}^{n} y_j)$$

Points (i) to (iii) in Assumption (A.2) are standard and need no comment [see Debreu (1962) for some relaxations of these hypotheses]. Point (iv) establishes that, for every $(\mathbf{p}, \bar{\mathbf{y}})$ in $\mathbb{P} \times \mathbb{R}^{\ell n}$, each consumer's wealth is a continuous mapping, and that total wealth equals the value of initial endowments plus total profits.

Remark.- Note that we have defined the *jth* firm's pricing rule as a mapping ϕ_j applying $\mathbb{P} \times \mathfrak{F}$ into $\mathbb{P}$, rather than into $\mathbb{R}^{\ell}$ (which would have been a more general setting). Yet, it is clear that under assumptions (A.1) and (A.2) there is no loss of generality in such a definition.

Consider now the following definitions:

<u>Definition.-</u> We shall say that $\phi_j: \mathbb{P} \times \mathfrak{F} \rightarrow \mathbb{P}$ is a **Regular Pricing Rule**, if ϕ_j is an upper hemicontinuous correspondence, with nonempty, closed and convex values.

<u>Definition.-</u> We shall say that $\phi_j : \mathbb{P} \times \mathfrak{F} \dashrightarrow \mathbb{P}$ is a **Pricing Rule with Bounded Losses**, if a scalar $\alpha_j \leq 0$ exists such that, for each $(\mathbf{p}, \bar{\mathbf{y}})$ in $\mathbb{P} \times \mathfrak{F}$,

$$ q_j \, y_j \geq \alpha_j, \quad \forall \ q_j \in \phi_j(\mathbf{p}, \bar{\mathbf{y}}) $$

Remark.- The combination of the notions of bounded-losses and regularity implies a non-trivial structure on the pricing rule. In particular, it prevents a firm from setting:

$$ \phi_j(\mathbf{p}, \bar{\mathbf{y}}) \equiv \{ q^o \} $$

(constant) for all $(\mathbf{p}, \bar{\mathbf{y}})$ in $\mathbb{P} \times \mathfrak{F}$ (which would easily destroy any possibility of equilibria). The reader is encouraged to think about the nature of this implication [Bonnisseau & Cornet (1988 a, Remark 2.6) will help].

For a given $\mathbf{p} \in \mathbb{P}$, let $m_i(\mathbf{p})$ denote the minimum value of $\mathbf{p} \, c_i$, with $c_i \in C_i$ (that is, m_i denotes the minimum worth at prices $\mathbf{p}$ of a feasible consumption bundle for the *ith* consumer). This is clearly a continuous function (by virtue of the maximum Theorem). The next definition incorporates a restriction on the distribution of wealth which provides us with a straightforward *survival assumption*.

<u>Definition.-</u> Let ϕ_1, ϕ_2, ..., ϕ_n stand for the n firms' pricing rules. We shall say that a wealth structure, $(r_1, ..., r_m)$ is **compatible with firms' behaviour**, if there exists an arbitrary small scalar $\delta > 0$, such that, for each consumer and for every production equilibrium $(p, \bar{y})$ in $\bigcap_{j=1}^{n} \phi_j(p, \bar{y}) \times \mathfrak{F}$,

$$r_i(p, \bar{y}) \geq m_i(p) + \delta$$

Thus we say that the distribution of wealth is compatible with firms' behaviour if, in a production equilibrium, each consumer's budget set has a nonempty interior.

<u>Definition.-</u> We shall say that a price vector $p^* \in \mathbb{P}$, and an allocation $[(c_i^*), \bar{y}^*]$, yield a **Market Equilibrium** if the following conditions are satisfied:

(α) For each $i = 1, 2, ..., m$, c_i^* maximizes u_i over the set of points c_i in C_i such that:

$$p \, c_i \leq r_i(p, \bar{y})$$

(β) For every $j = 1, 2, ..., n$, the jth firm is in equilibrium, that is,

$$p^* \in \bigcap_{j=1}^{n} \phi_j(p^*, \bar{y}^*)$$

(γ) $\sum_{i=1}^{m} c_i^* - \sum_{j=1}^{n} y_j^* \leq \omega$, and:

$$\sum_{i=1}^{m} c_{it}^{*} - \sum_{j=1}^{n} y_{jt}^{*} < \omega_t \implies p_t^{*} = 0$$

That is, a Market Equilibrium is a situation in which: (a) Consumers maximize their preferences subject to their budget constraints; (b) Every firm is in equilibrium; and (c) All markets clear.

Let $\mathbb{E}$ denote the class of economies just described, that is, market economies satisfying assumptions (A.1) and (A.2). The main result of this Chapter goes as follows:

THEOREM IV,2,1.- Let E stand for an economy in $\mathbb{E}$. A Market Equilibrium exists when firms follow regular pricing rules with bounded losses, and the wealth structure is compatible with firms' behaviour.

(The proof is given in Section IV,4)

IV.3.- PRICING RULES

This Section is devoted to presenting a family of equilibrium models which are particular cases of the one developed in Section IV.2. These specific models illustrate the flexibility of the pricing rule approach for the analysis of general equilibrium, and add some flesh to the abstract framework above.

Let us start by introducing the family of loss-free pricing rules, and concentrate on the case of private ownership market economies.

<u>Definition.-</u> We shall say that $\phi_j : \mathbb{P} \times \mathfrak{J} \longrightarrow \mathbb{P}$ is a **Loss-Free Pricing Rule**, if for each $(\mathbf{p}, \bar{\mathbf{y}})$ in $\mathbb{P} \times \mathfrak{J}$, all $\mathbf{q}_j$ in $\phi_j(\mathbf{p}, \bar{\mathbf{y}})$, we have:

$$\mathbf{q}_j \, \mathbf{y}_j \geq 0$$

Let $(A.1^*)$ denote a modification of assumption $(A.1)$ consisting in adding the following requirement:

$$Y_j \cap \mathbb{R}_+^\ell = \{ 0 \} \quad , \quad \forall \; j$$

(that is, we assume furthermore that firms cannot produce without using up some inputs, and that inactivity is always feasible).

Let $(A.2^*)$ denote a modification of assumption $(A.2)$ consisting of substituting point (iv) by the following:

(iv*) (a) $r_i(p, \bar{y}) = p\,\omega_i + \sum_{1=1}^{n} \theta_{ij}\,p\,y_j$ (with $\sum_{1=1}^{n} \omega_i = \omega$,

$\sum_{j=1}^{m} \theta_{ij} = 1$).

(b) $\omega_i \in int.C_i$.

Call now $\mathbb{E}^*$ to set of private ownership market economies satisfying assumptions (A.1*) and (A.2*). The following Corollary turns out to be an immediate consequence of the Theorem:

Corollary.- Let E stand for an economy in $\mathbb{E}^*$. A Market Equilibrium exists when firms follow regular and loss-free pricing rules.

Thus, in the context of private ownership market economies which satisfy (A.1*) and (A.2*), loss-free pricing rules constitute a special case of pricing rules for which *any wealth structure turns out to be compatible with firms' behaviour.*

We shall now consider three cases which provide prominent examples of regular and loss-free pricing rules: Profit maximization, average cost pricing and voluntary trading [see Bonnisseau & Cornet (1988 a, Section 3), and Dehez & Drèze (1988 a, Lemma 1)].

(A) <u>Profit maximization (under convex technologies)</u>

When technologies are convex, profit maximization can be defined in terms of the following pricing rule:

$$\phi_j^{PM}(p, \bar{y}) \equiv \{\, q \in R_+^\ell \ / \ q \, y_j \geq q \, y_j' \,, \ \forall \, y_j' \in Y_j \,\}$$

This pricing rule associates to each efficient production plan, the set of prices which <u>support</u> it as the most profitable one (that is, in this case ϕ_j coincides with the inverse supply mapping).

Under assumption (A.1*), this is obviously a *loss-free* pricing rule (since $0 \in Y_j$ for each j); it is also easy to deduce that ϕ_j^{PM} is *regular* (the maximum theorem implies the upper hemicontinuity, whilst the convexity of Y_j brings about the convex valuedness). *Thus, in particular, the existence of a Walrasian equilibrium is obtained as a Corollary of this Theorem.*

(B) <u>Average cost-pricing</u>

Average cost-pricing is a pricing rule with a long tradition in economics (both in positive and normative analysis). It can be formulated as follows[2]:

$$\phi_j^{AC}(p, \bar{y}) \equiv \{ \, q \in \mathbb{R}_+^\ell \,\, / \,\, q \, y_j = 0 \, \}$$

that is, this rule associates to each efficient production plan for the *jth* firm, those prices yielding null profits.

Under assumption (A.1*), ϕ_j^{AC} is a loss-free and regular pricing rule (by reasoning such as that used above). Hence, the Theorem provides an implicit existence result for those economies where firms are instructed to obtain zero profits.

Average cost-pricing belongs to a family of loss-free and regular pricing rules, whose associated equilibria may be difficult to sustain, since some firms may find it profitable to deviate from the equilibrium production plans (i.e., think of decreasing returns to scale). The next pricing rule intends to overcome such a difficulty, by requiring cost minimization [the reader may well consult Scarf (1986) and Dehez & Drèze (1988 b) for a discussion of this type of problem].

---

[2] This expression corresponds to the case where $y_j \neq 0$. For $\bar{y}$ such that $y_j = 0$, the *jth* firm's pricing rule must be defined as the closed convex hull of the following set:

$$\{ \, q \in \mathbb{R}_+^\ell \,\, / \,\, \exists \, \{q^\nu, y_j^\nu\} \subset \mathbb{R}_+^\ell \times [\mathfrak{F}_j \setminus 0] \, , \, \text{such that,}$$

$$\{q^\nu, y^\nu\} \longrightarrow (q, 0), \text{ with } q^\nu y^\nu = 0 \, \}$$

(C) Voluntary trading

Dehez & Drèze (1988 a) introduce the notion of *voluntary trading* as a way of extending the notion of competitive equilibria to a context whereby firms behave as quantity takers, and there may be increasing returns to scale [see Dierker & Neuefeind (1988) for a different approach]. This pricing rule is defined as follows:

$$\phi_j^{VT}(p, \bar{y}) \equiv \{ q \in \mathbb{R}_+^\ell \ / \ q \ y_j \geq q \ y, \ \forall \ y \in Y_j \ \text{with} \ y \leq y_j^+ \}$$

(where y_j^+ denotes a vector in $\mathbb{R}_+^\ell$ with coordinates max. $\{ 0, y_{jh} \}$, for $h = 1, 2, \ldots, \ell$).

The main feature of this pricing rule is that at those prices "it is not more profitable for the producers to produce less. Thus at an equilibrium, producers maximize profits subject to a sales constraint" [Cf. Dehez & Drèze (1988 a, p. 210)]. These authors show that under assumption (A.1*) ϕ_j^{VT} is a loss-free and regular pricing rule which collapses to profit maximization under convex technologies.

Finally, let us consider a pricing rule from which most of the existence results on general equilibrium in nonconvex environments originated: the marginal (cost) pricing. This pricing rule shares, together with voluntary trading, the feature that it coincides with profit maximization when production sets are convex.

D) Marginal (Cost) Pricing

The nowadays standard definition of marginal pricing is the following:

$$\phi_j^{MP}(\mathbf{p}, \bar{\mathbf{y}}) \equiv N_{Y_j}(\mathbf{y}_j) \cap \mathbb{P}$$

where $N_{Y_j}(\mathbf{y}_j)$ denotes Clarke's normal cone to Y_j at $\mathbf{y}_j$.[3]

The basic idea behind the marginal pricing is to associate to each point in the boundary of Y_j its gradient (whose generalization corresponds to Clarke's normal cone), so that the necessary conditions for optimality are fulfilled[4].

---

[3] To define Clarke's normal cone we have to start with the definition of a tangent cone. To do that, let Y be a closed subset of $\mathbb{R}^\ell$ and $\mathbf{y} \in Y$. Then, the tangent cone $T_Y(\mathbf{y})$ [in the sense of Clarke (1975)], to Y at $\mathbf{y}$ consists of all vectors $\mathbf{v} \in \mathbb{R}^\ell$ such that, for all sequences $\{\mathbf{y}^\nu\} \subset Y$, and $\{t^\nu\} \subset (0, +\infty)$ converging to $\mathbf{y}$ and 0, respectively, there exists a sequence $\{\mathbf{v}^\nu\}$ converging to $\mathbf{v}$ such that, for ν large enough,

$$\mathbf{y}^\nu + t^\nu \mathbf{v}^\nu \in Y$$

Clarke's normal cone $N_Y(\mathbf{y})$ is then defined by polarity as follows:

$$N_Y(\mathbf{y}) \equiv \{\mathbf{p} \in \mathbb{R}^\ell \;/\; \mathbf{p}\,\mathbf{v} \leq 0, \;\; \forall\, \mathbf{v} \in T_Y(\mathbf{y})\}$$

[Cf. Bonnisseau & Cornet (1988 a, p. 135)].

[4] It is known that, in the absence of convexity, marginal cost pricing equilibria may not even satisfy (aggregate) production efficiency, unless one considers specific models [see also the problem raised in Jouini's (1988) paper]. There are however results showing that this pricing rule allows for the decentralization of Pareto efficient allocations [see for instance Guesnerie (1975), Bonnisseau & Cornet (1988 b)].

It can be shown [e.g. Cornet (1990)] that under assumption (A.1), ϕ_j^{MP} is a regular pricing rule, so that the Theorem also applies to this case, whenever the wealth structure is compatible with firms' behaviour. Bonnisseau & Cornet (1988 a, Lemma 4.2) show that assuming marginal pricing with bounded losses implies that Y_j is star-shaped [more precisely, assuming that $q_j y_j \geq \alpha_j \quad \forall \; y_j \in \mathfrak{F}_j$, for all $q_j \in \mathcal{N}_{Y_j}(y_j) \cap \mathbb{P}$, turns out to be equivalent to assuming that $\forall \; y_j \in Y_j$, $[\alpha_j e, \; y_j] \subset Y_j$, where e stands for the unit vector, $e \equiv (1, 1, \ldots, 1)$].

IV.4.- THE EXISTENCE OF MARKET EQUILIBRIUM

For each $j = 1, 2, \ldots, n$, define a mapping $g_j : \mathbb{P} \times \mathfrak{F} \longrightarrow \mathbb{R}^\ell$ such that it associates to every $(p, \bar{y})$ in $\mathbb{P} \times \mathfrak{F}$ the set of points t_j which solve the following program:

$$\text{Min.} \quad \text{dist.}[\, t_j, y_j \,]$$
$$t_j$$
$$\text{s.t.:}$$
$$r_i[(p, y_1, \ldots, t_j, \ldots, y_n) \geq m_i(p) + \delta \, , \, \forall \, i$$
$$p \, t_j \geq \alpha_j$$

It is easy to check that, for each $(p, \bar{y})$ in $\mathbb{P} \times \mathfrak{F}$, there is a unique solution to this program, which varies continuously with $(p, \bar{y})$. Thus, for each j, g_j is actually a continuous function. We shall write $g(p, \bar{y}) \equiv \sum\limits_{j=1}^{n} g_j(p, \bar{y})$, which obviously is a continuous function of its arguments.

Let us call now $\mathscr{A}'(\omega)$ to the following set:

$$\{\, [(c_i)\,(y_j)] \in \prod\limits_{i=1}^{m} C_i \times \mathfrak{F} \,/\, \sum\limits_{i=1}^{m} c_i - \omega \leq \sum\limits_{j=1}^{n} g_j(p, \bar{y}), \, \forall \, p \in \mathbb{P} \,\}$$

which is a nonempty and compact subset of $\mathbb{R}^{\ell(m+n)}$, under assumptions (A.1) and (A.2). Let $\mathfrak{F}'_j$ denote the projection of $\mathscr{A}'(\omega)$ on $\mathfrak{F}_j$, with $\mathfrak{F}' \equiv \prod\limits_{j=1}^{n} \mathfrak{F}'_j$, and let $\mathfrak{F}^*_j$ stand for a compact subset of $\mathfrak{F}_j$ such that $\mathfrak{F}'_j \subset \text{int.} \mathfrak{F}^*_j$, and call $\mathfrak{F}^* \equiv \prod\limits_{j=1}^{n} \mathfrak{F}^*_j$.

By construction, for each $(p, \bar{y})$ in $\mathbb{P} \times \mathfrak{F}^*$, for every i,

$$r_i[p, g_1(p, \bar{y}), \ldots, g_n(p, \bar{y})] \geq m_i(p) + \delta$$

Remark.- Observe that if we do not impose the restriction $\mathbf{p} \, t_j \geq \alpha_j$, for all j (which corresponds to the bounded losses assumption), the set $\mathcal{A}'(\omega)$ would not be bounded, and the reasoning below could not be applied.

The following Lemma is a direct consequence of assumption (A.1), and hence the proof will be omitted [see Bonnisseau & Cornet (1988 a, Lemma 5.1)].

Lemma IV,4,1.- Let Y_j be a production set satisfying (A.1), and let $\mathfrak{J}^*_j$ stand for a compact subset of $\mathfrak{J}_j$, such that $\mathfrak{J}'_j \subset \mathrm{int}.\mathfrak{J}^*_j$. Then, $\mathfrak{J}^*_j$ can be made homeomorphic to a simplex:

$$X_j = \{ \ x_j \in \mathbb{R}^\ell_+ \ / \ \sum_{1=1}^{\ell} x_{ij} = 1 \ \}$$

so that the set of points in $\mathfrak{J}'_j$ are mapped into the interior of X_j.

For each $j = 1, 2, ..., n$, let h_j denote the (continuous) inverse mapping which associates to every x_j in X_j a unique y_j in $\mathfrak{J}^*_j$. Consider now the following sets:

$$\mathbb{X} \equiv \prod_{j=1}^{n} X_j$$

$$\Delta \equiv \mathbb{P} \times \mathbb{X}$$

$\bar{x} = (x_1, ..., x_n)$ will denote a point in $\mathbb{X}$. We shall write:

$$\hat{g}_j(p, \bar{x}) \equiv g_j[p, h_j(x_j)]$$

$$\hat{g}(p, \bar{x}) \equiv \sum_{j=1}^{n} \hat{g}_j(p, \bar{x})$$

which are obviously continuous functions on Δ.

Let now $\hat{E}$ denote an economy identical to E in all respects except for consumers' budget sets. More precisely, define

$$\hat{\xi}(p, \bar{x}) \equiv \hat{d}(p, \bar{x}) - \{\omega\} ,$$

where:

$$\hat{d}(p, \bar{x}) \equiv \sum_{i=1}^{m} \hat{d}_i(p, \bar{x}),$$

and $\hat{d}_i(p, \bar{x})$ stands for the set of solutions to the program:

$$\text{Max.} \quad u_i(c_i)$$

$$\text{s.t.:}$$
$$c_i \in C_i$$
$$p\,c_i \leq r_i[p, \hat{g}_1(p, \bar{x}), ..., \hat{g}_n(p, \bar{x})]$$

Let $h(\bar{x}) \equiv [h_1(x_1), h_2(x_2), ..., h_n(x_n)]$, and define a mapping $\Gamma: \Delta \longrightarrow \mathbb{R}^{\ell(1+n)}$ as follows:

$$\Gamma(p, \bar{x}) \equiv \begin{bmatrix} \hat{\xi}(p, \bar{x}) - \hat{g}(p, \bar{x}) \\ p - \phi_1[p, h(\bar{x})] \\ p - \phi_2[p, h(\bar{x})] \\ \cdots\cdots\cdots \\ p - \phi_n[p, h(\bar{x})] \end{bmatrix}$$

Remark.- Notice that Γ is a correspondence consisting of $(1 + n)$ ℓ-vector mappings. The first one corresponds to the "excess supply" mapping of $\hat{E}$, whilst each of the remaining n can be interpreted as the difference between the price vector proposed by the auctioneer and those acceptable for each firm.

We are ready now to present our main result:

THEOREM IV,2,1.- Let E stand for an economy in $\mathbb{E}$. A Market Equilibrium exists when firms follow regular pricing rules with bounded losses, and the wealth structure is compatible with firms' behaviour.

Proof.-

Let $\hat{E}$ stand for the economy defined above. Observe that assumption (A.2) and the definition of $\hat{g}_j$ all imply that for all $i = 1,2,\ldots, m$, the mapping $\gamma_i : \Delta \longrightarrow C_i$ given by:

$$\gamma_i(p, \bar{x}) = \{ c_i \in C_i \; / \; p \, c_i \leq r_i[p, \hat{g}_1(p, \bar{x}), \ldots, \hat{g}_n(p, \bar{x})] \}$$

is continuous in $(p, \bar{x})$ [Debreu (1959, 4.8 (1))], with nonempty, compact and convex values. Therefore, since preferences are assumed to be continuous and convex, for each pair $(p, \bar{x}) \in \Delta$, every $\hat{d}_i$ will be an upper-hemicontinuous correspondence (the maximum theorem applies here), with nonempty, compact and convex values. Consequently, $\hat{\xi}$ inherits these properties and, by hypothesis and the way of constructing the $\hat{g}$ mapping, this also applies for Γ.

Thus, Γ is an upper-hemicontinuous correspondence, with nonempty, compact and convex values, applying a compact and convex set, $\Delta \subset \mathbb{R}_+^{\ell(1+n)}$ into $\mathbb{R}^{\ell(1+n)}$. Then, Theorem II,3,1 ensures the existence of points $(p^*, \bar{x}^*) \in \Delta$, $(z^*, v^*) \in \Gamma(p^*, \bar{x}^*)$ such that,

$$(p^*, \bar{x}^*)\,(z^*, v^*) \geq (p, \bar{x})\,(z^*, v^*)$$

for every pair $(p, \bar{x})$ in Δ. In particular,

$$(p^*, \bar{x}^*)\,(z^*, v^*) \geq (p, \bar{x}^*)\,(z^*, v^*) \quad , \; \forall\, p \in \mathbb{P} \qquad [1]$$

$$(p^*, \bar{x}^*)\,(z^*, v^*) \geq (p^*, \bar{x})\,(z^*, v^*) \quad , \; \forall\, \bar{x} \in \mathbb{X} \qquad [2]$$

From [1] it follows that $p^*\, z^* \geq p\, z^*$, for all $p \in \mathbb{P}$, which implies:

$$p^*\, z^* = \max_j\, z_j^*$$

Therefore, the Walras Law implies that $p^*\, z^* = 0$, that is,

$$\max_j\, z_j^* = 0 \;,$$

and hence, $z^* \leq 0$ [that is, this allocation belongs to $\mathcal{A}'(\omega)$], with $p_s^* = 0$ whenever $z_s^* < 0$.

Similarly, from [2] it follows that $\bar{x}^*\, v^* \geq \bar{x}\, v^*$, for all $\bar{x}$ in $\mathbb{X}$, and hence for each j we get: $x_j^*\, v_j^* \geq x_j\, v_j^*$ for all x_j in X_j. Consequently, for each j,

$$x_j^*\, v_j^* = \max_i\, v_{ij}^*$$

which implies that either $v_{kj}^* = \{ \max_i\, v_{ij}^* \}$, or $x_{kj}^* = 0$. Since $z^* \leq 0$ implies that the corresponding allocation belongs to $\mathcal{A}'(\omega)$, by construction, each x_j^* must be a point in the interior of X_j, that is, $v_{kj}^* = \{ \max_i\, v_{ij}^* \} \; \forall\, k, \; \forall\, j$. Now, since for each j, $v_j^* \equiv p^* - q_j^*$

consists of the difference between two points in $\mathbb{P}$ (for some $q_j^* \in \phi_j[\mathbf{p}^*, h(\bar{\mathbf{x}}^*)])$, it must be the case that $\mathbf{v}_j^* = 0$ for all j, that is,

$$\mathbf{p}^* \in \bigcap_{j=1}^{n} \phi_j[\mathbf{p}^*, h(\mathbf{x}^*)]$$

Therefore, a market equilibrium for $\hat{E}$ exists.

Observe now that since ϕ_j is a pricing rule with bounded losses, and that the wealth structure is compatible with firms' behaviour, it follows that:

$$\mathbf{p}^* h_j(\mathbf{x}_j^*) \geq \alpha_j \quad , \ \forall \ j$$

$$r_i[\mathbf{p}^*, h(\mathbf{x}^*)] \geq m_i(\mathbf{p}^*) + \delta \quad , \qquad \forall i$$

Therefore, $\hat{g}_j(\mathbf{p}^*, \bar{\mathbf{x}}^*) = h_j(\mathbf{x}_j^*)$, and consequently

$$0 \geq \mathbf{z}^* \in \xi(\mathbf{p}^*,\bar{\mathbf{x}}^*) - \sum_{j=1}^{n} h_j(\mathbf{x}_j^*)$$

that is, $\mathbf{p}^*$ actually yields a Market Equilibrium for E.

The proof is in this way completed.

Remark.- Observe that the proof allows us to interpret the auctioneer as proposing those prices and production plans such that, they maximize the value of the "excess demand" and minimize the distance between each pricing rule and the proposed prices.

Chapter V:

Further Applications

V.1.- INTRODUCTION

This Chapter is devoted to the analysis of three different models, which provide further applications of the results in Part One.

The first one (Section V,2) deals with the same distributive problem discussed in Chapter III, but in a more general context. The three new ingredients of the problem are the following:

a) The existence of both "goods" and "bads" will explicitly be considered.

b) Consumers' consumption sets will be modelled taking into account the presence of lower bounds.

c) We shall allow the planner to face "balance restrictions" (that is, having to allocate the whole amount of the goods being distributed).

The existence of egalitarian allocations in this general setting is the main result of Section V,2.

Section V,3 analyzes the existence of Lindahl equilibrium in a model with several public goods and price externalities. The main purpose of the model in this Section consists of showing an application of the abstract Theorem II,4,1.

Section V,4 deals with the solvability of nonlinear input-output models. We consider extensions of the standard open Leontief model in which input functions are continuous, and satisfy a minimal productivity requirement.

V.2.- EGALITARIAN ALLOCATIONS: THE GENERAL CASE

We shall present here a more general setting in which the existence of egalitarian allocations can be shown to exist. This model corresponds to the work developed in Herrero & Villar (1990).

This new model exhibits two main differences with respect to that in Chapter III. The first one is that a more general class of consumption sets is considered (which implies that the notion of egalitarian allocations should be suitably redefined). The second one refers to the possibility that *the planner may face "balance restrictions"* (there may be institutional or strategical reasons requiring that it should be distributed exactly what is available of certain commodities; this adds more structure to the feasible set which will consequently shrink).

Throughout this Section we mantain the same notation that in Sections III,2 and III,3.

Consider a distributive problem involving n agents and k commodities. Without loss of generality we shall assume that commodities 1,2, ..., h are "goods", whilst commodities h+1, h+2, ..., k are efforts. Following the standard convention, goods will be denoted by nonnegative numbers and efforts by nonpositive ones.

Let now $X_j \subset \mathbb{R}_+^h \times \mathbb{R}_-^{k-h}$ stand for the jth agent consumption set, and let X stand for the cartesian product of the n agents' consumption sets. Let $\omega \in \mathbb{R}^h_+ \times \mathbb{R}^{k-h}_-$ be the bundle of commodities to be distributed among the n agents, and let $K = \{1,2,\dots, k\}$. We shall denote by τ a subset of K which identifies those commodities subject to "balance restrictions" (that is, those commodities which have to be fully distributed). The set of *attainable distributions* can then be written as,

$$\mathcal{A}(\omega, \tau) = \{\ x \in X \ / \sum_{j=1}^{n} x_j \leq \omega \ \& \ i \in \tau \ ==> \ \sum_{j=1}^{n} x_{ij} = \omega_i \ \}$$

A *Distributive Problem*, $\mathfrak{D}$, can be characterized by :

$$\mathfrak{D} = [\ X, \ u, \ \mathcal{A}(\omega, \tau)\ ]$$

with implicit parameters n (the number of agents) and k (the number of commodities).

A consistent extension of the notion of egalitarian allocations requires taking into account that there may be boundary problems (due to the existence of lower bounds in consumption sets). In order to do so, let us define a **subsistence bundle** for the jth agent as a point $x_j \in X_j$ such that there is no point in X_j with smaller components. Let B_j denote the set of subsistence bundles for the jth agent, and X^+_j its complement in X_j, that is,

$$B_j = \{\ x_j \in X_j \ / \ y \in \mathbb{R}^k \ \& \ y \ll x_j \ ==> \ y \notin X_j \ \}$$

$$X^+_j = X_j \setminus B_j$$

Let now $\mathcal{E}(\mathfrak{D})$ denote the following set:

$$\{ \; x \in \mathcal{A}(\omega, \tau) \; / \; u_j(x) > u_t(x) \; \& \; x_j \in X_j^+ \; ==> \; x_j \leq 0 \; \& \; x_t \geq 0 \; \}$$

$\mathcal{E}(\mathfrak{D})$ consists of feasible points such that those agents with higher welfare receive no goods and those agents with lower welfare provide no efforts (unless all high welfare agents are kept at a subsistence level). Trivially, any feasible allocation strictly equalizing all agents welfare levels belongs to $\mathcal{E}(\mathfrak{D})$. When there are only goods, and $X_j = \mathbb{R}_+^k$ for all j, $\mathcal{E}(\mathfrak{D})$ coincides with that in Section III,2.

Egalitarian allocations are defined as before:

Definition.- Let $\mathfrak{D} = [\; X, \; u, \; \mathcal{A}(\omega, \tau) \;]$ be given. A point $\mathbf{x}^*$ will be called an **egalitarian allocation** if:

    (a) $\mathbf{x}^* \in \mathcal{E}(\mathfrak{D})$

    (b) $\min_j \; u_j(\mathbf{x}^*) \geq \min_j \; u_j(x), \quad \forall \; x \in \mathcal{E}(\mathfrak{D})$

That is, $\mathbf{x}^*$ is egalitarian if it is an allocation in $\mathcal{E}(\mathfrak{D})$ for which the lowest welfare value attainable is maximum.

Consider now the following assumptions:

S.1.- For all $j = 1,2,\ldots, n$, $X_j \subset \mathbb{R}^k$ is a nonempty, closed and convex set, bounded from below. Furthermore, if $x_j \in X_j$, and r is a point in $\mathbb{R}_+^h \times \mathbb{R}_-^{k-h}$ such that $r > x_j$, then $r \in X_j$.

S.2.- $\mathcal{A}(\omega, \tau)$ is nonempty.

S.3.- $u_j:X \longrightarrow \mathbb{R}$ is a continuous function, $\forall j$.

Assumptions (S.1) to (S.3) generalize those in Section III,2 in a natural way.

The following result is obtained:

Theorem V,2,1.- [Herrero & Villar (1990)]

Let $\mathfrak{D}$ be a distributive problem satisfying assumptions (S.1), (S.2) and (S.3). Then, there exists an egalitarian allocation.

Proof.-

Define a vector function $F:\mathcal{A}(\omega, \tau) \longrightarrow \mathbb{R}^{nk}$, as follows:

$$F_{ij}(x) = u_j(x) \quad , \quad i = 1,2,\ldots, k; \; j = 1,2,\ldots, n$$

Assumptions (S.1) to (S.3) imply that F is a regular mapping, applying a nonempty compact and convex subset of $\mathbb{R}^{nk}$ on $\mathbb{R}^{nk}$. Thus, Theorem II,3,1 ensures the existence of a point x' in $\mathcal{A}(\omega, \tau)$ such that, for all $x \in \mathcal{A}(\omega, \tau)$,

$$\sum_{j=1}^{n} \sum_{i=1}^{k} x'_{ij} \, u_j(x') \leq \sum_{j=1}^{n} \sum_{i=1}^{k} x_{ij} \, u_j(x')$$

That implies that x' is an allocation associating the smallest feasible values of x_{ij} to those agents with higher welfare. In other words, x' is a point in $\mathcal{E}(\mathfrak{D})$.

It is easy to check that $\mathcal{E}(\mathfrak{D})$ is a compact set. Hence, we can obtain an egalitarian allocation as a solution to the following program:

$$\text{Max.} \quad g(\mathbf{x}) = \min_{j} u_j(\mathbf{x})$$

s.t.

$$\mathbf{x} \in \mathcal{E}(\mathfrak{D})$$

which by construction is well defined.

Theorem V,2,1 ensures that we can always distribute a bundle of k commodities (including "goods" and "bads"), among n agents in a way such that: (i) All agents which receive some goods will have the same welfare values, with no agent having a smaller one; (ii) if there are individuals with higher welfare, then they get no goods and provide all efforts (except possibly those "high welfare" individuals getting subsistence bundles at $\mathbf{x}*$); and (iii) there is no allocation satisfying (i) and (ii) and yielding a higher minimum value.

Observe that this is an existence result much more general than Theorem III,2,1, since: (a) all kind of consumption externalities are allowed for (provided utility functions are continuous); and (b) the feasible set may exhibit "balance restrictions".

The generality of the model above (where the only relevant restriction was the continuity of utility functions), does not allow us to go beyond existence. It is clear that if we assume that individual utilities are freely disposable, egalitarian allocations are Pareto optimal (since this property implies the comprehensiveness of the utility possibility set). Moreover, when assumption (A.2) of Section III,2 also holds, and $\tau = \emptyset$, Corollary II,2,1,2 applies again and ensures the optimality of egalitarian allocations.

Remark.- For a detailed analysis of the optimality of egalitarian allocations in this general setting, see Herrero & Villar (1990).

V.3.- THE EXISTENCE OF LINDAHL EQUILIBRIA IN A MODEL WITH SEVERAL PUBLIC GOODS AND PRICE EXTERNALITIES[1]

Consider an economy in which there are k public goods and a single private one [see Foley (1967), Milleron (1972), Roberts (1974) or Cornwall (1984, Ch. 6) for details]. We want to analyze the existence of Lindahl equilibria when prices may affect utilities.

The possibility of prices affecting utilities has mostly been analyzed in private goods economies [see for instance Arrow & Hahn (1971, 6.1)]. In the context of public goods economies this seems a very natural framework: my willingness to pay may depend on what others are going to pay.

There are n consumers, each one endowed with ω_j units of the private good ($j = 1, 2, \dots, n$). $X_j \subset \mathbb{R}_+^{k+1}$ stands for the jth consumer consumption set. Consumers' welfare depends on the amounts of public and private goods they enjoy, and on the vector of Lindahl prices. Hence we can write the jth consumer's utility function as follows:

$$u_j : X_j \times \mathbb{R}_+^{nk} \dashrightarrow \mathbb{R} \qquad , \quad j = 1, 2, \dots, n$$

where $u_j(x_j, y, p)$ makes explicit that the jth consumer' welfare depends on the private good she consumes, x_j, the amounts of public

_____

[1] Cf. Herrero & Villar (1991)

goods provided, $\mathbf{y} = (y_1, y_2, ..., y_k)$, and the vector of Lindahl prices,

$$\mathbf{p} = (p_{ij}) \quad , \quad i = 1, 2, ..., k \quad ; \quad j = 1, 2, ..., n$$

where p_{ij} denotes the *jth* consumer contribution to the provision of the *ith* public good.

Concerning consumers we shall assume:

A.1.- For each $j = 1, 2, ..., n$:

(a) X_j is a nonempty, compact and convex subset of $\mathbb{R}_+^{k+1}$.

(b) u_j is continuous, quasi-concave in its arguments, and increasing in x_j.

(c) $\omega_j \in \text{rel.int.} X_j$.

This is a standard assumption. In particular, let us point out that the compactness of X_j is assumed for the sake of simplicity, and that the insatiability hypothesis in (b) implies that the private good will always have a positive exchange value (so that it can be taken as the *numéraire*).

For each vector of Lindahl prices, $\mathbf{p} \in \mathbb{R}_+^{nk}$, the *jth* consumer's demand is obtained from the solution to the following program:

$$\text{Max. } u_j(x_j, y^j, \mathbf{p})$$

s.t.

$$x_j + \sum_{i=1}^{k} p_{ij} y_i^j = \omega_j$$

For each given $p = \bar{p}$, let $\xi_j(\bar{p})$ stand for the set of solutions to this program. Under assumption (A.1), the following properties follow:

(i) $\xi_j(\bar{p})$ is nonempty, compact and convex. (ii) ξ_j is upper hemicontinuous (the maximum theorem applies here).

Let now $d_j : \mathbb{R}_+^{nk} \longrightarrow \mathbb{R}_+^k$, $j = 1, 2, \ldots, n$, stand for the projection of the demand mapping ξ_j on the public goods space (that is, $d_j(p)$ is the *jth* consumer's demand for public goods). Since u_j is increasing in x_j, there is no loss of information when the demand for the private good is ignored. Furthermore, d_j preserves properties (i) and (ii) above[2].

We shall suppose that each public good is competitively produced by single-production firms using the private good as an input, under constant returns to scale. The private good is taken as the *numéraire*.

Each firm producing the *ith* public good faces an output price given by

$$P_i = \sum_{j=1}^{n} P_{ij}$$

---

[2] Since each d_j may be understood as the intersection of two nonempty and closed-valued upper hemicontinuous correspondences, ξ_j and γ_j, where $\gamma_j(p) = X_j \cap \mathbb{R}_+^k$, for all p [see Hildenbrand (1974, Prop. 2a, p. 231)].

For the sake of simplicity we shall choose units so that the supply correspondence for the *i*th public good, i = 1,2,..., k, is only defined if $p_i \leq 1$.

Summarizing:

A.2.- Public goods are competitively produced by single-production firms. The aggregate supply correspondence for the *i*th public good, i = 1,2,..., k , is given by:

$$s_i(p_i) = \begin{cases} 0, & \text{when } p_i < 1 \\ [0, +\infty), & \text{when } p_i = 1 \\ \text{undefined}, & \text{when } p_i > 1 \end{cases}$$

Then, a *Lindahl Equilibrium* with (possibly) positive supply of public goods is a pair $(\mathbf{y}^*, \mathbf{p}^*)$, $\mathbf{y}^* \in \mathbb{R}_+^k$, $\mathbf{p}^* \in \mathbb{R}_+^{nk}$, such that:

(i) For all i = 1,2,..., k, $\sum_{j=1}^{n} p_{ij}^* = 1$.

(ii) For each j = 1,2,..., n, there is some $y^j \in d_j(\mathbf{p}^*)$ satisfying the following two requirements:

(ii,a) $y_i^j \leq y_i^*$

(ii,b) $y_i^j < y_i^*$ implies $p_{ij}^* = 0$

for all i = 1,2,..., k.

That is, $\mathbf{p}^*$ yields a Lindahl equilibrium if it equalizes the demand for the *i*th public good, i = 1,2,..., k, for every consumer with a positive personalized price (that is, a positive contribution to the provision of this public good). Notice that the budget constraint ensures the feasibility of such allocation.

The next result follows:

THEOREM V,3,1.- Let an economy satisfying assumptions **(A.1)** and **(A.2).**

Then, there exists a Lindahl equilibrium for this economy.

<u>Proof.-</u>

First notice that we may restrict our search for equilibrium points to the cartesian product of k unit simplexes, $S = \prod_{i=1}^{k} S_i$, where:

$$S_i = \{ p_i \in \mathbb{R}_+^n \ / \ \sum_{j=1}^{n} p_{ij} = 1 \}$$

Each of these simplexes describes how the total cost of a public good is distributed among the n consumers. Moreover, every demand correspondence, d_j, is upper-hemicontinuous with nonempty, compact and convex values. Then, defining a mapping Γ as $\Gamma(p) \equiv - \prod_{j=1}^{n} d_j(p)$, the result follows from Theorem II,4,1.

Finally, the Walras Law ensures that the market for the private good will also be in equilibrium.

■

V.4.- NONLINEAR INPUT-OUTPUT MODELS

Consider a Leontief economy, that is, an economy producing n commodities by means of produced commodities and a single primary input[3] (labour, say), in absence of joint production. Let $x \in \mathbb{R}^n_+$ denote the vector of gross outputs, and $T(x)$ the vector of (aggregate) inputs required in order to produce x (observe that this formulation allows for the presence of production externalities, since each individual T_i is taken to be a function of x). Finally, $d \in \mathbb{R}^n_+$ is a parameter vector representing the final demand of produced commodities. An equilibrium for the quantity system is defined as a solution to the following equation:

$$x = T(x) + d \qquad [1]$$

Remark.- Note that the standard linear input-output model is a particular case of this one, with $T(x) = Ax$, where A is a nonnegative n-square matrix.

Consider now the following assumptions:

---

[3] We consider a single primary input according to the tradition in this literature. Yet, as far as primary factors do not limit production possibilities, the existence result below also applies when there is a number of them.

A.1.- $T: \mathbb{R}^n_+ \longrightarrow \mathbb{R}^n_+$ is a continuous function.

A.2.- For each $d \in \mathbb{R}^n_+$ there exists some β (depending on d) such that for every x in $S(\beta) = \{ z \in \mathbb{R}^n_+ \ / \ \sum_{i=1}^{n} z_i = \beta \}$, there exists some index j such that, $x_j > 0$ and $x_j \geq T_j(x) + d_j$.

These assumptions generalize those nonlinear input-output models where the continuity of input functions is assumed[4] [see for instance Fujimoto (1980), Lahiri & Pyatt (1980), Chander (1983), Fujimoto, Herrero & Villar (1985), Silva (1986), Fujimoto & Villar (1987)]. Assumption (A.2) is a "weak productivity" restriction; it means that for any final demand we can always find high enough output levels (measured by β), so that the corresponding net output vectors cannot be strictly smaller than the given final demand.

Remark.- In the linear case, $T(x) = Ax$, assumption (A.2) turns out equivalent to the following conditions: (i) $(I - A)$ is a P-matrix [Gale & Nikaido (1965)]; and (ii) there exists some x' such that $x' - Ax' \gg 0$ [see Karamardian (1972), Silva (1984, I,3)].

The next result is obtained:

---

[4] Some results on the solvability of nonlinear input-output models, dispensing with the continuity assumption appear in Fujimoto (1986), Villar & Herrero (1989).

THEOREM V,4,1.- Under assumptions (A.1) and (A.2), for all $d \in \mathbb{R}_+^n$ there exists $x* \in \mathbb{R}_+^n$, such that: $x* = T(x*) + d$.

Proof.-

For each given d in $\mathbb{R}_+^n$ define $F(x; d) = x - T(x) - d$, and consider the following complementarity problem:

$$F(x; d) \geq 0$$

$$x\, F(x; d) = 0 \qquad\qquad [2]$$

$$x \geq 0$$

Assumptions (A.1) and (A.2) imply that F is a continuous vector function, semimonotone over $S(\beta)$. Furthermore, the structure of the mapping implies that $F_j(x) \leq 0$ whenever $x_j = 0$. Then, (ii) of Corollary II,3,2,1 ensures the existence of $x* \in \mathbb{R}_+^n$ such that $F(x*) = 0$ for each given d.

∎

A different approach to the solvability of this model is by making use of the properties of Z-Functions. For that, substitute assumptions (A.1) and (A.2) by the following:

A.3.- $T:\mathbb{R}_+^n \longrightarrow \mathbb{R}_+^n$ is continuous and isotone [i.e., $x \geq y$ implies $T(x) \geq T(y)$].

The isotoness property says that higher outputs require higher inputs. This is also a property satisfied by the linear input-output model.

It is now immediate to check that, under assumption (A.3), the mapping $F(x; d) \equiv x - T(x) - d$ is a continuos Z-Function. Then, the next result is obtained:

Theorem V,4,2.- Let $x' \in \mathbb{R}^n_+$ be a point such that $x' - T(x') \geq 0$. Under assumption (A.3), for every $d \in \mathbb{R}^n_+$ such that $d \leq x' - T(x')$, there exists an efficient solution to system [1].

Proof.-

Let $F(x; d) \equiv x - T(x) - d$, and call $d' \equiv x' - T(x')$. Under assumption (A.3) F is a continuous Z-Function for each given d. Furthermore, if $0 \leq d \leq d'$ the conditions of Theorem II,2,1 are satisfied, and therefore the complementarity problem [2] will have an efficient solution, $x^* \in \mathbb{R}^n_+$, which corresponds to an efficient solution to system [1], by reasoning as in Theorem V,4,1..

Corollary V,4,2,1.- Under assumption (A.3) suppose the following conditions hold:

(i) There exists $x'' \in \mathbb{R}^n_+$ such that $x'' \gg T(x'')$.

(ii) T is subhomogeneous, i.e., $\forall \lambda \geq 1$, $T(\lambda x) \leq \lambda T(x)$.

Then, for every $d \in \mathbb{R}^n_+$ there exists an efficient solution to system [1].

Proof.-

First notice that, for $\lambda \geq 1$, $d(\lambda) \equiv \lambda x'' - T(\lambda x'')$ is strictly increasing in λ. Therefore, Theorem V,4,2 ensures the existence of an efficient solution for every $d \in \mathbb{R}^n_+$.

■

Remark.- Herrero & Silva (1991) analyze the equivalence between these mappings and the strong solvability of system [1], and discuss the conditions under which the uniqueness of such solutions can be ensured. Fujimoto, Herrero & Villar (1985) develop a sensitivity analysis for this type of models.

REFERENCES

Archibald, G.C. & Donaldson, D. (1976), Nonpaternalism and the Basic Theorems of Welfare Economics, **Canadian Journal of Economics**, 9 : 492-507.

Archibald, G.C. & Donalson, D. (1979), Notes on Economic Equality, **Journal of Public Economics**, 12 : 205-214.

Arrow, K.J. (1963), **Social Choice and Individual Values**, 2nd Ed., Yale University Press, New Haven.

Arrow, K.J. (1977), Extended Sympathy and the Possibility of Social Choice, **American Economic Review**, Supplementary Issue of the Proceedings: 219-225.

Arrow, K.J. & Hahn, F.H. (1971), **General Competitive Analysis**, Holden Day, San Francisco.

Atkinson, A.B. (1970), On the Measurement of Inequality, **Journal of Economic Theory**, 2 : 244-263.

Baiocchi, C. & Capelo, A. (1984), **Variational and Quasi-Variational Inequalities: Applications for Free-Boundary Problems**, John Wiley. New York.

Baumol, W.J. (1986), **Superfairness. Applications and Theory**, The MIT Press, Cambridge Ma.

Beato, P. & Mas-Colell, A. (1985), On Marginal Cost Pricing with Given Tax-Subsidy Rules, **Journal of Economic Theory**, 37 : 356-365.

Bergstrom, T.C. (1970), A "Scandinavian Consensus" Solution for Efficient Income Distributions among Nonmalevolent Consumers, **Journal of Economic Theory**, 2 : 383-398.

Berman, A. & Plemmons, R.J. (1979), **Nonnegative Square Matrices in the Mathematical Sciences**, Academic Press, New York.

Bidard, C. (1989), Equilibrium with a Qualitative Walras' Law, **Journal of Economic Theory**, 47 : 203-205.

Böhm, V.(1986), Existence of Equilibria with Price Regulation, in W. Hildenbrand & A. Mas-Colell (Eds.), 1986.

Bonnisseau, J.M., (1988), On Two Existence Results of Equilibria in Economies with Increasing Returns, **Journal of Mathematical Economics**, 17 : 193-207.

Bonnisseau, J.M. & Cornet, B. (1988 a), Existence of Equilibria when Firms follow Bounded Losses Pricing Rules, **Journal of Mathematical Economics**, 17 : 119-147.

Bonnisseau, J.M. & Cornet, B. (1988 b), Valuation Equilibrium and Pareto Optimum in Non-Convex Economies, **Journal of Mathematical Economics**, 17 : 293-308.

Bonnisseau, J.M. & Cornet, B. (1990 a), Existence of Marginal Cost Pricing Equilibria in Economies with Several Nonconvex Firms, **Econometrica**, 58 : 661-682.

Bonnisseau, J.M. & Cornet, B. (1990 b), Existence of Marginal Cost Pricing Equilibria: The Nonsmooth Case, **International Economic Review**, 31 : 685-708.

145

Brown, D.J., Heal, G., Khan, M.A. & Vohra, R. (1986), On a General Existence Theorem for Marginal Cost Pricing Equilibria, **Journal of Economic Theory**, 38 : 371-379.

Border, K.C. (1985), **Fixed Point Theorems with Applications to Economics and Game Theory**, Cambridge University Press, New York.

Boskin, M.J. & Sheshinky, E. (1978), Optimal Income Redistribution when Individual Welfare Depends on Relative Income, **Quarterly Journal of Economics**, 92 : 589-602.

Brennan, G. (1973), Pareto Desirable Redistributions: The Case of Malice and Envy, **Journal of Public Economics**, 2 : 173-183.

Browder, F.E. (1968), The Fixed Point Theory of Multi-Valued Mappings in Topological Vector Spaces, **Mathematische Annalen**, 177 : 283-301.

Chan, D. & Pang, J.S. (1982), The Generalized Quasi-Variational Inequality Problem, **Mathematics of Operation Research**, 7 : 211-222.

Chander, P. (1983), The Nonlinear Input-Output Model, **Journal of Economic Theory**, 30 : 219-229.

Clarke, F. (1975), Generalized Gradients and Applications, **Transactions of the American Mathematical Society**, 205 : 247-262.

Corchón, L. (1988), Cost-Prices with Variable Returns, **Metroeconomica**, 40 : 93-99.

Cornet, B. (1988), General Equilibirum Theory and Increasing Returns, **Journal of Mathematical Economics,** 17 : 103-118.

Cornet, B. (1990), Existence of Equilibria in Economies with Increasing Returns, in B. Cornet & H. Tulkens (Eds.), **Contributions to Economics and Operations Research: The XXth Anniversary of the C.O.R.E.,** The MIT Press, Cambridge Ma.

Cornwall, R.E. (1984), **Introduction to the Use of General Equilibrium Analysis,** North Hollan, Amsterdam.

Cottle, R.W. (1966), Nonlinear Programs with Positively Bounded Jacobian, **SIAM Journal on Applied Mathematics,** 14 : 147-157.

Cottle, R.W. (1980), Some Recent Developments in Linear Complementarity Theory, Chapter 7 in Cottle *et al.* Eds., 1980.

Cottle, R.W., Giannessi, F. & Lions, J.L., Eds. (1980), **Variational Inequalities and Complementary Problems Theory and Applications,** John Wiley & Sons, Chichester.

Crawford, V. (1977), A Game of Fair Division, **Review of Economic Studies,** 44 : 235-247.

Dafermos, S. (1980), Traffic Equilibria and Variational Inequalities, **Transportation Science,** 14 : 43-54.

Dafermos, S. & Nagurney, A. (1987), Oligopolistic and Competitive Behaviour of Spatially Separated Markets, **Regional Science and Urban Economics,** 17 : 245-254.

Dantzig, G.B. & Jackson, P.L. (1980), Pricing Underemployed Capacity in a Linear Economic Model, Chapter 9 inCottle et al. Eds., 1980.

D'Aspremont, C. (1985), Axioms for Social Welfare Orderings, Chapter 2 in Hurwicz *et al.* Eds., 1985.

D'Aspremont, C. & Gevers, L. (1977) Equity and Informational Basis of Collective Choice, **Review of Economic Studies,** 44 : 199-209.

Debreu, G. (1959), **Theory of Value,** Yale University Press, New Haven.

Debreu, G. (1962), New Concepts and Techniques for Equilibrium Analysis, **International Economic Review,** 3 : 257-273.

Debreu, G. (1982), Existence of Competitive Equilibrium, Chapter 15 in **Handbook of Mathematical Economics,** vol. II, edited by K.J. Arrow and M.D. Intriligator, North-Holland, Amxterdam.

Dehez, P. (1988), Rendements d'Echelle Croissants et Equilibre General, **Revue d'Economie Politique,** 98 : 765-800.

Dehez, P. & Drèze, J. (1988 a), Competitive Equilibria with Quantity-Taking Producers and Increasing Returns to Scale, **Journal of Mathematical Economics,** 17 : 209-230.

Dehez, P. & Drèze, J. (1988 b), Distributive Production Sets and Equilibria with Increasing Returns, **Journal of Mathematical Economics,** 17 : 231-248.

Deschamps, R. & Gevers, L. (1978), Leximin and Utilitarian Rules: A Joint Characterization, **Journal of Economic Theory,** 17: 143-163.

Dierker, E, Guesnerie, R. & Neuefeind, W. (1985), General Equilibrium where some Firms Follow Special Pricing Rules, **Econometrica,** 53 : 1369-1393.

Dierker, H. & Neuefeind, W. (1988), Quantity Guided Price Setting, **Journal of Mathematical Economics,** 17 : 249-259.

Fan, K. (1961) A Generalization of Tychonoff's Fixed Point Theorem, **Mathematische Annalen,** 142 : 305-310.

Fan, K. (1969), Extensions of Two Fixed Points Theorems of F.E. Browder, **Mathematical Zeitschrift,** 112 : 234-240.

Florenzano, M. (1981), **L'Equilibre Economique General Transitif et Intransitif: Problemes d'Existence,** Editions du CNRS, Paris.

Foley, D.K. (1967),Resource Allocation and the Public Sector, **Yale Economic Essays,** 7 : 45-98.

Fujimoto, T. (1980), Global Strong Le Chatelier-Samuelson Principle, **Econometrica,** 48 : 1667-1674.

Fujimoto, T. (1984), An Extension of Tarski's Fixed Point Theorem and its Application to Isotone Complementarity Problems, **Mathematical Programming,** 28 : 116-118.

Fujimoto, T. (1986), Nonlinear Leontief Models in Abstract Spaces, **Journal of Mathematical Economics,** 15 : 151-156

Fujimoto, T., Herrero, C. & Villar, A. (1985), A Sensitivity Analysis in a Nonlinear Input-Output Model, **Zeitschrift für Nationalökonomie,** 45 : 23-26.

Fujimoto, T. & Villar, A. (1987), Nonlinear Leontief Models without the Monotonicity of Input Functions, **The Kagawa University Economic Review,** 59 (4) : 31-40.

Gabay, D. & Moulin, H. (1980), On the Uniqueness and Stability of Nash Equilibria in Non-Cooperative Games, in A. Bensoussan, P. Kleindorfer & C. Tapiero, Eds., **Applied Stochastic Control in Econometrics and Management Science,** North Holland, Amsterdam, 1980.

Gale, D. (1955), The Law of Supply and Demand, **Mathematica Scandinavica,** 3 : 155-169.

Gale, D. & Nikaido, H. (1965), Jacobian Matrix and Global Univalence Mapping, **Mathematische Annalen,** 159 : 81-93.

Gowda, M.S. & Pang, J.S. (1990), Some Existence Results for Multivalued Complementarity Problems, **Mathematics of Operations Research,** forthcoming.

Guesnerie, R. (1975), Pareto Optimality in Nonconvex Economies, **Econometrica,** 43 : 1-29.

Gutierrez, J.M. & Herrero, C. (1990), Lagrangean Conditions for General Optimization Problems with Applications to Consumer Theory, **A Discusión,** wp 90-02, University of Alicante.

Habetler, G.J. & Price, A.L. (1971), Existence Theory for Generalized Nonlinear Complementary Problems, **Journal of Optimization Theory and Applications,** 7 : 223-239.

Hammond, P. (1977), Dual Interpersonal Comparisons of Utility and the Welfare Economics of Income Distribution, **Journalof Public Economics,** 7 : 143-163.

Harker, P. T. (1984), A Variational Inequality Approach for the Determination of Oligopolistic Market Equilibrium, **Mathematical Programming,** 30, 105-111.

Harker, P. T., Ed. (1985), **Spatial Price Equilibrium: Advances in Theory, Computation and Application,** Springer-Verlag, Berlin.

Harker, P. T. & Pang, J. S. (1990), Finite Dimensional Variational Inequality and Nonlinear Complementarity Problems: A Survey of Theory, Algorithms and Applications, **Mathematical Programming,** 48 : 161-220.

Hart, S. & Mas-Colell, A. (1989), Potential, Value and Consistency, **Econometrica,** 57 : 589-614.

Hartman, P. & Stampachia, G. (1966), On Some Non Linear Eliptic DifferencialEquations, **Acta Mathematica,** 115 : 271-310.

Herrero, C. & Silva, J.A. (1991), On the Equivalence between Solvability and Strict Semimonotonicity of some Systems Involving Z-Functions, **Mathematical Programming,** 49 : 371-179.

Herrero, C. & Subiza, B. (1991), A Characterization of Acyclic Preferences on Countable Sets, **A Discusión**, w.p. 9101.

Herrero, C. & Villar, A. (1988 a), General Equilibrium in a Nonlinear Leontief Framework, **The Manchester School**, 56 : 159-166.

Herrero, C. & Villar, A. (1988 b), A Characterization of Economies with the Nonsubstitution Property, **Economics Letters**, 26 : 147-162.

Herrero, C. & Villar, A. (1990), Egalitarian Allocations in the Presence of Consumption Externalities, **A Discusión**, w.p. n° 34, University of Alicante.

Herrero, C. & Villar, A. (1991), Vector Mappings with Diagonal Images, **Mathematical Social Sciences**, forthcoming.

Hildenbrand, W. (1974), **Core and Equilibria of a Large Economy**, Princeton University Press, Princeton.

Hildenbrand, W. & Mas-Colell, A., Eds. (1986), **Contributions to Mathematical Economics. Essays in Honor of Gérard Debreu**, North-Holland, Amsterdam.

Hochman, H.M. & Rodgers, J.D. (1969), Pareto Optimal Redistributions, **American Economic Review**, 59 : 542-557.

Hurwicz, L., Schmeidler, D. & Sonnenschein, H., Eds. (1985), **Social Goals and Social Organization. Essays in Memory of Elisha Pazner**, Cambridge University Press, New York.

Ichiischi, T. (1983), **Game Theory for Economic Analysis**, Academic Press, New York.

Jouini, E. (1988), A Remark on Clarke's Normal Cone and the Marginal Cost Pricing Rule, **Journal of Mathematical Economics**, 17 : 309-315.

Kalai, E. (1977), Proportional Solutions to Bargaining Situations: Interpersonal Utility Comparisons, **Econometrica**, 45 : 1623-1630.

Kalai, E. (1985), Solutions to the Bargaining Problem, Chapter 3 in Hurwicz *et al.* Eds., 1985.

Kalai, E. & Smorodinski, M. (1975), Other Solutions to Nash's Bargaining Problem, **Econometrica**, 53 : 513-518.

Kamiya, K. (1988), Existence and Uniqueness of Equilibria with Increasing Returns, **Journal of Mathematical Economics**, 17 : 149-178.

Karamardian, S. (1971), Generalized Complementarity Problem, **Journal of Optimization Theory and Applications**. 8 : 161-167.

Karamardian, S. (1972), The Complementarity Problem, **Mathematical Programming**, 2 : 107-129.

Kolm, S.Ch. (1972), **Justice et Equité**, Editions du CNRS, Paris.

Knaster, B., Kuratowski, K. & Mazurkiewicz, S. (1929), Ein Beweis des Fixpunktsatze fur n-Dimensionale Simplexes, **Fundamenta Mathematica**, 14 : 132-137.

Lahiri, S. & Pyatt, G. (1980), On the Solutions of Scale-Dependent Input-Output Models, **Econometrica**, 48 : 1827-1830.

Lemke, C.E. (1980), A Survey of Complementarity Theory, Chapter 15 in Cottle *et al.*, Eds., 1980.

Mas-Colell, A. (1974), An Equilibrium Existence Theorem without Complete or Transitive Preferences, **Journal of Mathematical Economics**, 1 : 237-246.

Mas-Colell, A. (1987), **Lecciones sobre la Teoría del Equilibrio con Rendimientos Crecientes**, Segundas Lecciones Germán Bernácer, Valencia, Generalitat Valenciana.

McLinden, L. (1980), The Complementarity Problem for Maximal Monotone Multifunctions, Chapter 17 in Cottle *et al.* Eds., 1980.

Michael, E. (1956), Continuous Selections I, **Annals of Mathematics**, 63: 361-382.

Milleron, J.C. (1972), Theory of Value with Public Goods: A Survey Article, **Journal of Economic Theory**, 5 : 419-477.

Moré, J.J. (1974 a), Classes of Functions and Feasibility Conditions in Nonlinear Complementarity Problems, **Mathematical Programming**, 6 : 327-338.

Moré, J.J. (1974 b), Coercivity Conditions in Nonlinear Complementarity Problems, **SIAM Review**, 16 : 1-16.

Moré, J.J. & Rheinboldt, W. (1973), On P- and S-Functions and Related Classes of n-Dimensional Mappings, **Linear Algebra and Its Applications**, 6 : 45-68.

Moulin, H. (1988), **Axioms of Cooperative Decision Making**, Cambridge University Press, New York.

Moulin, H. (1989), Fair Division under Joint Ownership: Recent Results and Open Problems, **Third Germán Bernácer Lectures**, University of Alicante.

Moulin, H. & Thomson, W. (1988), Can Everyone Benefit from Growth? Some Difficulties, **Journal of Mathematical Economis**, 17 : 339-345.

Myerson, R.G. (1977), Two Person Bargaining Problems and Comparable Utility, **Econometrica**, 45 : 1631-1637.

Nagurney, A. (1987), Competitive Equilibrium Problems, Variational Inequalities and Regional Science, **Journal of Regional Science**, 27 : 503-517.

Neuefeiend, W. (1980), Notes on Existence of Equilibrium Proofs and the Boundary Behaviour of Supply, **Econometrica**, 48 : 1831-1837.

Ng, Y.K. (1975), Bentham or Bergstrom?. Finite Sensibility, Utility Functions and Social Welfare Functions, **Review of Economic Studies**, 42 : 545-569.

Nieto, J. (1991), A Note on Egalitarian and Efficient Allocations with Consumption Externalities, **Journal of Public Economics**, forthcoming.

Nikaido, H. (1956), On the Classical Multilateral Exchange Problem, **Metroeconomica**, 8 : 135-145.

Ortega, J.M. & Rheinboldt, W. (1970), **Iterative Solutions of Nonlinear Equations in Several Variables**, Academic Press, New York.

Pazner, E. (1977), Pitfalls in the Theory of Fairness, **Journal of Economic Theory**, 14 : 458-466.

Peleg, B. (1967), Equilibrium Points for Open Acyclic Relations, **Canadian Journal of Mathematics**, 19 : 366-369.

Peris, J.E. & Villar, A. (1988), On the Solvability of Joint Production Leontief Models, **A Discusión**, w.p. n$^{\circ}$ 25, University of Alicante.

Rawls, J. (1971), **A Theory of Justice**, Harvard University Press, Cambridge Ma.

Ridell, R.C. (1981) Equivalence of Nonlinear Complementarity Problems and Least Element Problems in Banach Lattices, **Mathematics of Operations Research**, 6 : 462-474.

Roberts, D.J. (1974), The Lindahl Solution for Economies with Public Goods, **Journal of Public Economics**, 3 : 23-42.

Roberts, K.W.S. (1980 a), Possibility Theorems with Interpersonally Comparable Welfare Levels, **Review of Economic Studies**, 47 : 409-420.

Roberts, K.W.S. (1980 b), Interpersonal Comparability and Social Choice Theory, **Review of Economic Studies**, 47 : 421-439.

Roberts, K.W.S. (1980 c), Social Choice Theory: The Single and Multiple-Profile Approaches, **Review of Economic Studies**, 47: 441-450.

Rockafellar, R.T. (1980), Lagrange Multipliers and Variational Inequalities, Chapter 20 in Cottle *et al.* Eds., 1980.

Roemer, J. (1986), Equality of Resources Implies Equality of Welfare, **Quarterly Journal of Economics**, 100 : 215-244.

Roemer, J. (1988), Axiomatic Bargaining Theory in Economic Environments, **Journal of Economic Theory**, 45 : 1-31.

Roth, A.E. (1979), Proportional Solutions to the Bargaining Problem, **Econometrica**, 47 : 775-778.

Runciman, W.G. (1966), **Relative Deprivation and Social Justice**, Routledge, London.

Saigal, R. (1976), Extensions of the Generalized Complementarity Problem, **Mathematics of Operations Research**, 1 : 260-266.

Scarf, H.E. (1986), Notes on the Core of a Productive Economy, in W. Hildenbrand & A. Mas-Colell (Eds.), 1986.

Schall, L.D. (1972), Interdependent Utilities and Pareto Optimality, **Quarterly Journal of Economics**, 86 : 19-24.

Schmeidler, D. (1971), A Condition for the Completeness of Partial Preference Relations, **Econometrica**, 39 : 403-404.

Sen, A. (1970), **Collective Choice and Social Welfare**, North Holland, Amsterdam.

Sen, A. (1974), Rawls versus Bentham: An Axiomatic Examination of the Pure Distribution Problem, **Theory and Decision**, 4 : 301-309.

Sen, A. (1976), Poverty: An Ordinal Approach to Measurement, **Econometrica**, 44 : 219-231.

Sen, A. (1982), **Choice, Welfare and Measurement**, Basil Blackwell, Oxford.

Sen, A. (1986 a), Social Choice Theory, in K.J. Arrow & M. Intriligator Eds., **Handbook of Mathematical Economics**, vol. III, North Holland, Amsterdam, 1986.

Sen, A. (1986 b), Information and Invariance in Normative Choice, in W.P. Heller, R.M. Starr & D.A. Starret, Eds., **Social Choice and Public Decision Making. Essays in Honor of K.J. Arrow**, vol. I, Cambridge University Press, New York, 1980.

Shafer, W.J. (1974), The Nontransitive Consumer, **Econometrica**, 42 : 913-919.

Shafer, W.J. & Sonnenschein, H. (1975), Equilibrium in Abstract Economies without Ordered Preferences, **Journal of Mathematical Economics**, 2 : 345-348.

Shapley, L.S. (1973), On Balanced Games without Side Payments, in T.C. Hu & S.M. Robinson (Eds.), **Mathematical Programming**, Academic Press, New York, 1973.

Shapley, L. & Vohra, R. (1991), On Kakutani's Fixed Point Theorem, the K-K-M-S Theorem and the Core of a Balanced Game, **Economic Theory**, 1 : 108-116.

Silva, J.A. (1984), **Existencia de Soluciones Semipositivas para Sistemas Lineales y No Lineales Vinculados a Modelos de Leontief**, Doctoral Dissertation, University of Alicante.

Silva, J.A. (1986), Equivalent Conditions for the Solvability of Nonlinear Leontief Systems, **Metroeconomica**, 38 : 167-179.

Sloss, J.L. (1971), Stable Points of Directional Preference Relations, Technical Report n° 71-7, Operations Research House, Stanford University.

Sonnenschein, H. (1971), Demand Theory without Transitive Preferences, with Applications to the Theory of Competitive Equilibrium, Chapter 10 in J.S. Chipman *et al.* Eds., **Preferences, Utility and Demand**, Harcourt Brace Jovanovich, New York.

Suzumura, K. (1983), **Rational Choice, Collective Decisions and Social Welfare**, Cambridge University Press, Cambridge.

Tamir, A. (1974), Minimality and Complementarity Properties Associated with Z-Functions and M-Functions, **Mathematical Programming**, 7 : 17-31.

Tarski, A. (1955), A Lattice Theoretic Fixpoint Theorem and its Applications, **Pacific Journal of Mathematics**, 5 : 285-309.

Thomson, W. (1987), Equity Concepts in Economics, **mimeo**, University of Rochester.

Thomson, W. (1989), Cooperative Models of Bargaining, **mimeo**, University of Rochester, w.p. n° 177.

Thomson, W. & Varian, H. (1985), Theories of Justice Based on Symmetry, Chapter 4 in Hurwicz *et al*. Eds., 1985.

Tinbergen, J. (1975), **Income Distribution: Analysis and Policies,** North Holland, Amsterdam.

Varian, H,R. (1974), Equity, Envy and Efficiency, **Journal of Economic Theory,** 9 : 63-91.

Villar, A. (1988 a), Two Theorems on Variational Inequalities for Set-Valued Mappings, with Applications to Equilibrium Models, **CORE Discussion Paper,** n° 8840.

Villar, A. (1988 b), On the Existence of Optimal Allocations when Individual Welfare Depends on Relative Consumption, **Journal of Public Economics,** 36 : 387-397.

Villar, A. (1988 c), La Lógica de la Elección Social: Una Revisión de los Resultados Básicos, **Investigaciones Económicas,** 12 : 3-44.

Villar, A. (1990), Nonlinear Operators in Euclidean Spaces: An Elementary "Users Guide" for Economists, **Mathematical Social Sciences,** 19 : 281-292.

Villar, A. (1991), A General Equilibrium Model with Increasing Returns, **Revista Española de Economía,** 8 (forthcoming).

Villar, A. & Herrero, C. (1985), Un Modelo Input-Output No Lineal, **Revista Española de Economía,** 2 : 333-345.

Villar, A. & Herrero, C. (1989), V-Mappings: A New Class of Vector Functions Suitable for the Solvability of Complementarity Problems, **mimeo**, University of Alicante.

Vohra, R. (1988), On the Existence of Equilibria in a Model with Increasing Returns, **Journal of Mathematical Economics**, 17 : 179-192.

Walker, M. (1977), On the Existence of Maximal Elements, **Journal of Economic Theory**, 16 : 470-474.

Yaari, M.E. (1981), Rawls, Edgeworth, Shapley, Nash: Theories of Distributive Justice Re-Examined, **Journal of Economic Theory**, 24 : 1-39.

Lecture Notes in Economics and Mathematical Systems

For information about Vols. 1–210
please contact your bookseller or Springer-Verlag

Vol. 211: P. van den Heuvel, The Stability of a Macroeconomic System with Quantity Constraints. VII, 169 pages. 1983.

Vol. 212: R. Sato and T. Nôno, Invariance Principles and the Structure of Technology. V, 94 pages. 1983.

Vol. 213: Aspiration Levels in Bargaining and Economic Decision Making. Proceedings, 1982. Edited by R. Tietz. VIII, 406 pages. 1983.

Vol. 214: M. Faber, H. Niemes und G. Stephan, Entropie, Umweltschutz und Rohstoffverbrauch. IX, 181 Seiten. 1983.

Vol. 215: Semi-Infinite Programming and Applications. Proceedings, 1981. Edited by A.V. Fiacco and K.O. Kortanek. XI, 322 pages. 1983.

Vol. 216: H.H. Müller, Fiscal Policies in a General Equilibrium Model with Persistent Unemployment. VI, 92 pages. 1983.

Vol. 217: Ch. Grootaert, The Relation Between Final Demand and Income Distribution. XIV, 105 pages. 1983.

Vol 218: P. van Loon, A Dynamic Theory of the Firm: Production, Finance and Investment. VII, 191 pages. 1983.

Vol. 219: E. van Damme, Refinements of the Nash Equilibrium Concept. VI. 151 pages. 1983.

Vol. 220: M. Aoki, Notes on Economic Time Series Analysis: System Theoretic Perspectives. IX, 249 pages. 1983.

Vol. 221: S. Nakamura, An Inter-Industry Translog Model of Prices and Technical Change for the West German Economy. XIV, 290 pages. 1984.

Vol. 222: P. Meier, Energy Systems Analysis for Developing Countries. VI, 344 pages. 1984.

Vol. 223: W. Trockel, Market Demand. VIII, 205 pages. 1984.

Vol. 224: M. Kiy, Ein disaggregiertes Prognosesystem fur die Bundesrepublik Deutschland. XVIII, 276 Seiten. 1984.

Vol. 225: T.R. von Ungern-Sternberg, Zur Analyse von Märkten mit unvollständiger Nachfragerinformaton. IX, 125 Seiten. 1984.

Vol. 226: Selected Topics in Operations Research and Mathematical Economics. Proceedings, 1963. Edited by G. Hammer and D. Pallaschke IX, 478 pages. 1984.

Vol. 227: Risk and Capital. Proceedings, 1983. Edited by G. Bamberg and K. Spremann VII, 306 pages. 1984.

Vol. 228: Nonlinear Models of Fluctuating Growth. Proceedings, 1983. Edited by R.M. Goodwin, M. Krüger and A. Vercelli. XVII, 277 pages. 1984.

Vol. 229: Interactive Decision Analysis. Proceedings, 1983. Edited by M. Grauer and A.P. Wierzbicki. VIII, 269 pages. 1984.

Vol. 230: Macro-Economic Planning with Conflicting Goals. Proceedings, 1982. Edited by M. Despontin, P. Nijkamp and J. Spronk. VI, 297 pages. 1984.

Vol. 231: G.F. Newell, The M/M/8 Service System with Ranked Servers in Heavy Traffic. XI, 126 pages. 1984.

Vol. 232: L. Bauwens, Bayesian Full Information Analysis of Simultaneous Equation Models Using Integration by Monte Carlo. VI, 114 pages. 1984.

Vol. 233: G. Wagenhals, The World Copper Market. XI, 190 pages. 1984.

Vol. 234: B.C. Eaves, A Course in Triangulations for Solving Equations with Deformations. III, 302 pages. 1984.

Vol. 235: Stochastic Models in Reliability Theory Proceedings, 1984. Edited by S. Osaki and Y. Hatoyama. VII, 212 pages. 1984.

Vol. 236: G. Gandolfo, P.C. Padoan, A Disequilibrium Model of Real and Financial Accumulation in an Open Economy. VI, 172 pages. 1984.

Vol. 237: Misspecification Analysis. Proceedings, 1983. Edited by T.K. Dijkstra. V, 129 pages. 1984.

Vol. 238: W. Domschke, A. Drexl, Location and Layout Planning. IV, 134 pages. 1985.

Vol. 239: Microeconomic Models of Housing Markets. Edited by K. Stahl. VII, 197 pages. 1985.

Vol. 240: Contributions to Operations Research. Proceedings, 1984. Edited by K. Neumann and D. Pallaschke. V, 190 pages. 1985.

Vol. 241: U. Wittmann, Das Konzept rationaler Preiserwartungen. XI, 310 Seiten. 1985.

Vol. 242: Decision Making with Multiple Objectives. Proceedings, 1984. Edited by Y.Y. Haimes and V. Chankong. XI, 571 pages. 1985.

Vol. 243: Integer Programming and Related Areas. A Classified Bibliography 1981–1984. Edited by R. von Randow. XX, 386 pages. 1985.

Vol. 244: Advances in Equilibrium Theory. Proceedings, 1984. Edited by C.D. Aliprantis, O. Burkinshaw and N.J. Rothman. II, 235 pages. 1985.

Vol. 245: J.E.M. Wilhelm, Arbitrage Theory. VII, 114 pages. 1985.

Vol. 246: P.W. Otter, Dynamic Feature Space Modelling, Filtering and Self-Tuning Control of Stochastic Systems. XIV, 177 pages.1985.

Vol. 247: Optimization and Discrete Choice in Urban Systems. Proceedings, 1983. Edited by B.G. Hutchinson, P. Nijkamp and M. Batty VI, 371 pages. 1985.

Vol. 248: Pural Rationality and Interactive Decision Processes. Proceedings, 1984. Edited by M. Grauer, M. Thompson and A.P. Wierzbicki. VI, 354 pages. 1985.

Vol. 249: Spatial Price Equilibrium: Advances in Theory, Computation and Application. Proceedings, 1984. Edited by P.T. Harker. VII, 277 pages. 1985.

Vol. 250: M. Roubens, Ph. Vincke, Preference Modelling. VIII, 94 pages. 1985.

Vol. 251: Input-Output Modeling. Proceedings, 1984. Edited by A. Smyshlyaev. VI, 261 pages. 1985.

Vol. 252: A. Birolini, On the Use of Stochastic Processes in Modeling Reliability Problems. VI, 105 pages. 1985.

Vol. 253: C. Withagen, Economic Theory and International Trade in Natural Exhaustible Resources. VI, 172 pages. 1985.

Vol. 254: S. Müller, Arbitrage Pricing of Contingent Claims. VIII, 151 pages. 1985.

Vol. 255: Nondifferentiable Optimization: Motivations and Applications. Proceedings, 1984. Edited by V.F. Demyanov and D. Pallaschke. VI, 350 pages. 1985.

Vol. 256: Convexity and Duality in Optimization. Proceedings, 1984. Edited by J. Ponstein. V, 142 pages. 1985.

Vol. 257: Dynamics of Macrosystems. Proceedings, 1984. Edited by J.-P. Aubin, D. Saari and K. Sigmund. VI, 280 pages. 1985.

Vol. 258: H. Funke, Eine allgemeine Theorie der Polypol- und Oligopolpreisbildung. III, 237 pages. 1985.

Vol. 259: Infinite Programming. Proceedings, 1984. Edited by E.J. Anderson and A.B. Philpott. XIV, 244 pages. 1985.

Vol. 260: H.-J. Kruse, Degeneracy Graphs and the Neighbourhood Problem. VIII, 128 pages. 1986.

Vol. 261: Th.R. Gulledge, Jr., N.K. Womer, The Economics of Made-to-Order Production. VI, 134 pages. 1986.

Vol. 262: H.U. Buhl, A Neo-Classical Theory of Distribution and Wealth. V, 146 pages. 1986.

Vol. 263: M. Schäfer, Resource Extraction and Market Struucture. VI, 154 pages. 1986.

Vol. 264: Models of Economic Dynamics. Proceedings, 1983. Edited by H.F. Sonnenschein. VII, 212 pages. 1986.

Vol. 265: Dynamic Games and Applications in Economics. Edited by T. Basar. IX, 288 pages. 1986.

Vol. 266: Multi-Stage Production Planning and Inventory Control. Edited by S. Axsäter, Ch. Schneeweiss and E. Silver. V, 264 pages. 1986.

Vol. 267: R. Bemelmans, The Capacity Aspect of Inventories. IX, 165 pages. 1986.

Vol. 268: V. Firchau, Information Evaluation in Capital Markets. VII, 103 pages. 1986.

Vol. 269: A. Borglin, H. Keiding, Optimality in Infinite Horizon Economies. VI, 180 pages. 1986.

Vol. 270: Technological Change, Employment and Spatial Dynamics. Proceedings, 1985. Edited by P. Nijkamp. VII, 466 pages. 1986.

Vol. 271: C. Hildreth, The Cowles Commission in Chicago, 1939–1955. V, 176 pages. 1986.

Vol. 272: G. Clemenz, Credit Markets with Asymmetric Information. VIII,212 pages. 1986.

Vol. 273: Large-Scale Modelling and Interactive Decision Analysis. Proceedings, 1985. Edited by G. Fandel, M. Grauer, A. Kurzhanski and A.P. Wierzbicki. VII, 363 pages. 1986.

Vol. 274: W.K. Klein Haneveld, Duality in Stochastic Linear and Dynamic Programming. VII, 295 pages. 1986.

Vol. 275: Competition, Instability, and Nonlinear Cycles. Proceedings, 1985. Edited by W. Semmler. XII, 340 pages. 1986.

Vol. 276: M.R. Baye, D.A. Black, Consumer Behavior, Cost of Living Measures, and the Income Tax. VII, 119 pages. 1986.

Vol. 277: Studies in Austrian Capital Theory, Investment and Time. Edited by M. Faber. VI, 317 pages. 1986.

Vol. 278: W.E. Diewert, The Measurement of the Economic Benefits of Infrastructure Services. V, 202 pages. 1986.

Vol. 279: H.-J. Büttler, G. Frei and B. Schips, Estimation of Disequilibrium Modes. VI, 114 pages. 1986.

Vol. 280: H.T. Lau, Combinatorial Heuristic Algorithms with FORTRAN. VII, 126 pages. 1986.

Vol. 281: Ch.-L. Hwang, M.-J. Lin, Group Decision Making under Multiple Criteria. XI, 400 pages. 1987.

Vol. 282: K. Schittkowski, More Test Examples for Nonlinear Programming Codes. V, 261 pages. 1987.

Vol. 283: G. Gabisch, H.-W. Lorenz, Business Cycle Theory. VII, 229 pages. 1987.

Vol. 284: H. Lütkepohl, Forecasting Aggregated Vector ARMA Processes. X, 323 pages. 1987.

Vol. 285: Toward Interactive and Intelligent Decision Support Systems. Volume 1. Proceedings, 1986. Edited by Y. Sawaragi, K. Inoue and H. Nakayama. XII, 445 pages. 1987.

Vol. 286: Toward Interactive and Intelligent Decision Support Systems. Volume 2. Proceedings, 1986. Edited by Y. Sawaragi, K. Inoue and H. Nakayama. XII, 450 pages. 1987.

Vol. 287: Dynamical Systems. Proceedings, 1985. Edited by A.B. Kurzhanski and K. Sigmund. VI, 215 pages. 1987.

Vol. 288: G.D. Rudebusch, The Estimation of Macroeconomic Disequilibrium Models with Regime Classification Information. VII,128 pages. 1987.

Vol. 289: B.R. Meijboom, Planning in Decentralized Firms. X, 168 pages. 1987.

Vol. 290: D.A. Carlson, A. Haurie, Infinite Horizon Optimal Control. XI, 254 pages. 1987.

Vol. 291: N. Takahashi, Design of Adaptive Organizations. VI, 140 pages. 1987.

Vol. 292: I. Tchijov, L. Tomaszewicz (Eds.), Input-Output Modeling. Proceedings, 1985. VI, 195 pages. 1987.

Vol. 293: D. Batten, J. Casti, B. Johansson (Eds.), Economic Evolution and Structural Adjustment. Proceedings, 1985. VI, 382 pages.

Vol. 294: J. Jahn, W. Knabs (Eds.), Recent Advances and Historical Development of Vector Optimization. VII, 405 pages. 1987.

Vol. 295. H. Meister, The Purification Problem for Constrained Games with Incomplete Information. X, 127 pages. 1987.

Vol. 296: A. Börsch-Supan, Econometric Analysis of Discrete Choice. VIII, 211 pages. 1987.

Vol. 297: V. Fedorov, H. Läuter (Eds.), Model-Oriented Data Analysis. Proceedings, 1987. VI, 239 pages. 1988.

Vol. 298: S.H. Chew, Q. Zheng, Integral Global Optimization. VII, 179 pages. 1988.

Vol. 299: K. Marti, Descent Directions and Efficient Solutions in Discretely Distributed Stochastic Programs. XIV, 178 pages. 1988.

Vol. 300: U. Derigs, Programming in Networks and Graphs. XI, 315 pages. 1988.

Vol. 301: J. Kacprzyk, M. Roubens (Eds.), Non-Conventional Preference Relations in Decision Making. VII, 155 pages. 1988.

Vol. 302: H.A. Eiselt, G. Pederzoli (Eds.), Advances in Optimization and Control. Proceedings, 1986. VIII, 372 pages. 1988.

Vol. 303: F.X. Diebold, Empirical Modeling of Exchange Rate Dynamics. VII, 143 pages. 1988.

Vol. 304: A. Kurzhanski, K. Neumann, D. Pallaschke (Eds.), Optimization, Parallel Processing and Applications. Proceedings, 1987. VI, 292 pages. 1988.

Vol. 305: G.-J.C.Th. van Schijndel, Dynamic Firm and Investor Behaviour under Progressive Personal Taxation. X, 215 pages.1988.

Vol. 306: Ch. Klein, A Static Microeconomic Model of Pure Competition. VIII, 139 pages. 1988.

Vol. 307: T.K. Dijkstra (Ed.), On Model Uncertainty and its Statistical Implications. VII, 138 pages. 1988.

Vol. 308: J.R. Daduna, A. Wren (Eds.), Computer-Aided Transit Scheduling. VIII, 339 pages. 1988.

Vol. 309: G. Ricci, K. Velupillai (Eds.), Growth Cycles and Multisectoral Economics: the Goodwin Tradition. III, 126 pages. 1988.

Vol. 310: J. Kacprzyk, M. Fedrizzi (Eds.), Combining Fuzzy Imprecision with Probabilistic Uncertainty in Decision Making. IX, 399 pages. 1988.

Vol. 311: R. Färe, Fundamentals of Production Theory. IX, 163 pages. 1988.

Vol. 312: J. Krishnakumar, Estimation of Simultaneous Equation Models with Error Components Structure. X, 357 pages. 1988.

Vol. 313: W. Jammernegg, Sequential Binary Investment Decisions. VI, 156 pages. 1988.

Vol. 314: R. Tietz, W. Albers, R. Selten (Eds.), Bounded Rational Behavior in Experimental Games and Markets. VI, 368 pages. 1988.

Vol. 315: I. Orishimo, G.J.D. Hewings, P. Nijkamp (Eds), Information Technology: Social and Spatial Perspectives. Proceedings 1986. VI, 268 pages. 1988.

Vol. 316: R.L. Basmann, D.J. Slottje, K. Hayes, J.D. Johnson, D.J. Molina, The Generalized Fechner-Thurstone Direct Utility Function and Some of its Uses. VIII, 159 pages. 1988.

Vol. 317: L. Bianco, A. La Bella (Eds.), Freight Transport Planning and Logistics. Proceedings, 1987. X, 568 pages. 1988.

Vol. 318: T. Doup, Simplicial Algorithms on the Simplotope. VIII, 262 pages. 1988.

Vol. 319: D.T. Luc, Theory of Vector Optimization. VIII, 173 pages. 1989.

Vol. 320: D. van der Wijst, Financial Structure in Small Business. VII, 181 pages. 1989.

Vol. 321: M. Di Matteo, R.M. Goodwin, A. Vercelli (Eds.), Technological and Social Factors in Long Term Fluctuations. Proceedings. IX, 442 pages. 1989.

Vol. 322: T. Kollintzas (Ed.), The Rational Expectations Equilibrium Inventory Model. XI, 269 pages. 1989.

Vol. 323: M.B.M. de Koster, Capacity Oriented Analysis and Design of Production Systems. XII, 245 pages. 1989.

Vol. 324: I.M. Bomze, B.M. Pötscher, Game Theoretical Foundations of Evolutionary Stability. VI, 145 pages. 1989.

Vol. 325: P. Ferri, E. Greenberg, The Labor Market and Business Cycle Theories. X, 183 pages. 1989.

Vol. 326: Ch. Sauer, Alternative Theories of Output, Unemployment, and Inflation in Germany: 1960–1985. XIII, 206 pages. 1989.

Vol. 327: M. Tawada, Production Structure and International Trade. V, 132 pages. 1989.

Vol. 328: W. Güth, B. Kalkofen, Unique Solutions for Strategic Games. VII, 200 pages. 1989.

Vol. 329: G. Tillmann, Equity, Incentives, and Taxation. VI, 132 pages. 1989.

Vol. 330: P.M. Kort, Optimal Dynamic Investment Policies of a Value Maximizing Firm. VII, 185 pages. 1989.

Vol. 331: A. Lewandowski, A.P. Wierzbicki (Eds.), Aspiration Based Decision Support Systems. X, 400 pages. 1989.

Vol. 332: T.R. Gulledge, Jr., L.A. Litteral (Eds.), Cost Analysis Applications of Economics and Operations Research. Proceedings. VII, 422 pages. 1989.

Vol. 333: N. Dellaert, Production to Order. VII, 158 pages. 1989.

Vol. 334: H.-W. Lorenz, Nonlinear Dynamical Economics and Chaotic Motion. XI, 248 pages. 1989.

Vol. 335: A.G. Lockett, G. Islei (Eds.), Improving Decision Making in Organisations. Proceedings. IX, 606 pages. 1989.

Vol. 336: T. Puu, Nonlinear Economic Dynamics. VII, 119 pages. 1989.

Vol. 337: A. Lewandowski, I. Stanchev (Eds.), Methodology and Software for Interactive Decision Support. VIII, 309 pages. 1989.

Vol. 338: J.K. Ho, R.P. Sundarraj, DECOMP: an Implementation of Dantzig-Wolfe Decomposition for Linear Programming. VI, 206 pages.

Vol. 339: J. Terceiro Lomba, Estimation of Dynamic Econometric Models with Errors in Variables. VIII, 116 pages. 1990.

Vol. 340: T. Vasko, R. Ayres, L. Fontvieille (Eds.), Life Cycles and Long Waves. XIV, 293 pages. 1990.

Vol. 341: G.R. Uhlich, Descriptive Theories of Bargaining. IX, 165 pages. 1990.

Vol. 342: K. Okuguchi, F. Szidarovszky, The Theory of Oligopoly with Multi-Product Firms. V, 167 pages. 1990.

Vol. 343: C. Chiarella, The Elements of a Nonlinear Theory of Economic Dynamics. IX, 149 pages. 1990.

Vol. 344: K. Neumann, Stochastic Project Networks. XI, 237 pages. 1990.

Vol. 345: A. Cambini, E. Castagnoli, L. Martein, P Mazzoleni, S. Schaible (Eds.), Generalized Convexity and Fractional Programming with Economic Applications. Proceedings, 1988. VII, 361 pages. 1990.

Vol. 346: R. von Randow (Ed.), Integer Programming and Related Areas. A Classified Bibliography 1984–1987. XIII, 514 pages. 1990.

Vol. 347: D. Ríos Insua, Sensitivity Analysis in Multi-objective Decision Making. XI, 193 pages. 1990.

Vol. 348: H. Störmer, Binary Functions and their Applications. VIII, 151 pages. 1990.

Vol. 349: G.A. Pfann, Dynamic Modelling of Stochastic Demand for Manufacturing Employment. VI, 158 pages. 1990.

Vol. 350: W.-B. Zhang, Economic Dynamics. X, 232 pages. 1990.

Vol. 351: A. Lewandowski, V. Volkovich (Eds.), Multiobjective Problems of Mathematical Programming. Proceedings, 1988. VII, 315 pages. 1991.

Vol. 352: O. van Hilten, Optimal Firm Behaviour in the Context of Technological Progress and a Business Cycle. XII, 229 pages. 1991.

Vol. 353: G. Ricci (Ed.), Decision Processes in Economics. Proceedings, 1989. III, 209 pages 1991.

Vol. 354: M. Ivaldi, A Structural Analysis of Expectation Formation. XII, 230 pages. 1991.

Vol. 355: M. Salomon. Deterministic Lotsizing Models for Production Planning. VII, 158 pages. 1991.

Vol. 356: P. Korhonen, A. Lewandowski, J . Wallenius (Eds.), Multiple Criteria Decision Support. Proceedings, 1989. XII, 393 pages. 1991.

Vol. 358: P. Knottnerus, Linear Models with Correlated Disturbances. VIII, 196 pages. 1991.

Vol. 359: E. de Jong, Exchange Rate Determination and Optimal Economic Policy Under Various Exchange Rate Regimes. VII, 270 pages. 1991.

Vol. 360: P. Stalder, Regime Translations, Spillovers and Buffer Stocks. VI, 193 pages . 1991.

Vol. 361: C. F. Daganzo, Logistics Systems Analysis. X, 321 pages. 1991.

Vol. 362: F. Gehrels, Essays in Macroeconomics of an Open Economy. V, ...

Vol. 363: C. ... and Choice under Risk. VIII, 100 pages . 1991

Vol. 364: B. Horvath, Are Policy Variables Exogenous? XII, 162 pages. 1991.

Vol. 365: G. A Heuer, U. Leopold-Wildburger. Balanced Silverman Games on General Discrete Sets. V, 140 pages. 1991.

Vol. 366: J. Gruber (Ed.), Econometric Decision Models. Proceedings, 1989. VIII, 636 pages. 1991.

Vol. 367: M. Grauer, D. B. Pressmar (Eds.), Parallel Computing and Mathematical Optimization. Proceedings. V, 208 pages. 1991.

Vol. 368: M. Fedrizzi, J. Kacprzyk, M. Roubens (Eds.), Interactive Fuzzy Optimization. VII, 216 pages. 1991.

Vol. 369: R. Koblo, The Visible Hand. VIII, 131 pages.1991.

Vol. 370: M. J. Beckmann, M. N. Gopalan, R. Subramanian (Eds.), Stochastic Processes and their Applications. Proceedings, 1990. XLI, 292 pages. 1991.

Vol. 371: A. Schmutzler, Flexibility and Adjustment to Information in Sequential Decision Problems. VIII, 198 pages. 1991.

Vol. 372: J. Esteban, The Social Viability of Money. X, 202 pages. 1991.

Vol. 373: A. Billot, Economic Theory of Fuzzy Equilibria. XIII, 164 pages. 1992.

Vol. 374: G. Pflug, U. Dieter (Eds.), Simulation and Optimization. Proceedings, 1990. X, 162 pages. 1992.

Vol. 375: S.-J. Chen, Ch.-L. Hwang, Fuzzy Multiple Attribute Decision Making. XII, 536 pages. 1992.

Vol. 376: K.-H. Jöckel, G. Rothe, W. Sendler (Eds.), Bootstrapping and Related Techniques. Proceedings, 1990. VIII, 247 pages. 1992.

Vol. 377: A. Villar, Operator Theorems with Applications to Distributive Problems and Equilibrium Models. XVI, 160 pages. 1992.

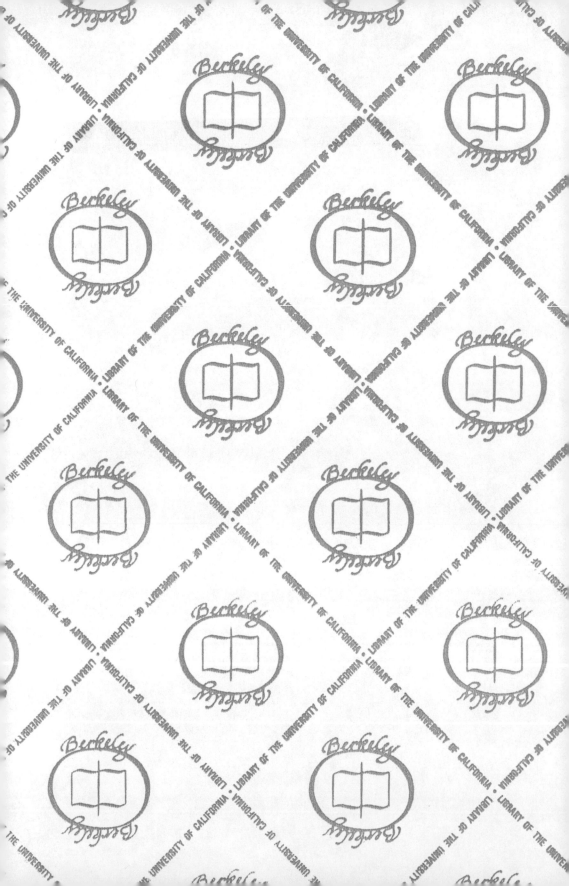